'This joyful, healing book is like having a loving, wise personal guide take your hand and bring you on a journey from where you are to where you want to be. You will feel better just as you read, and how deep you go is up to you – it's all here for the taking! You'll love it!'

JOE VITALE PhD, AUTHOR OF THE REMEMBERING PROCESS, *LIMITS* AND THE AWAKENING COURSE

'How to Be Well by Abby Wynne is a wonderful, grounded and practical guidebook to help us release those heavy energies that stop us from living a joyous life. A great read for anyone committed to lighting the world up with their presence.'

REBECCA CAMPBELL, AUTHOR OF LIGHT IS THE NEW BLACK

'In How to Be Well, Abby shares an array of wise and wonderful practical insights and exercises for enjoying holistic health in the real world. Not only will she help you to get well, but equally important, Abby's approach can help you to stay well for a wonderful life.'

SANDY C. NEWBIGGING, AUTHOR OF MIND CALM AND BODY CALM

'Abby Wynne has written a such a wonderful, easy-to-understand and practical guide on how to become well. The words that came to mind as I read were "grounding", "healing" and "nurturing". It actually felt like Abby's healing presence was in the room with me, taking me through each chapter! I just know this book will really help people on a fundamental level, and will therefore be a life changer for so many.'

CHARLOTTE REED, AUTHOR OF MAY THE THOUGHTS BE WITH YOU

'How to Be Well, from the deep and delightful Abby Wynne, is full of elegant exercises and powerful practices designed to cultivate and keep your wellness alive. Let Abby gently guide you on the path of permission and promise to a life free of stress and full of joy.'

NANCY LEVIN, BESTSELLING AUTHOR OF JUMP ... AND YOUR LIFE WILL APPEAR

'Have you ever been unwell and it simply makes no logical sense? Well, you need Abby's book. It's not the average self-help book, but a self-care book. It's like reading a personal letter from a friend with some back-up, real-life case studies and exercises that you will actually be bothered to do. If you're looking to lead an optimal life of vitality, Abby's book will guide you to make that a reality.'

BECKY WALSH, BROADCASTER, AUTHOR, INTUITIVE AND HUMAN DYNAMICS EXPERT

'This book has already earned itself a place on my treasure shelf. Abby's gentle and practical guidance makes it easy to get in touch with your true state of wellbeing, accept it with love and respect, and then lift yourself to happier and more comfortable levels of wellness. A gem of a book – clear, complete, achievable and welcoming in a way that can only be described as "Totally Abby".'

ANGIE GRACE, CREATOR OF THE BESTSELLING ANGIE GRACE COLOURING BOOKS

'Professionals in the healing arts and those who simply want an easy-to-follow, thoughtfully written guide to getting the best out of life are in for a real treat! How to Be Well is going to change the way in which people approach their own health, allowing compassion for one's personal history while teaching accountability for present day wellbeing. This book is an invaluable resource for those who are ready to create real and lasting changes in their lives.'

DR MARY HELEN HENSLEY, AUTHOR OF PROMISED BY HEAVEN

'You have in your hands a manual for deep self-care. Take a journey with Abby to explore all aspects of yourself, heal your relationships, learn how to stay well for life and reach your full potential. Whether you are new to energy work or an experienced therapist, the clarity of this book will ensure that you refer to and recommend it time and time again. Abby firmly places the power within your hands. As she so rightly says, "Your journey to wellness starts with you." So, what are you waiting for? Dive in and Be Well.'

KATE MARILLAT, CO-AUTHOR OF TRANSFORM YOUR BELIEFS, TRANSFORM YOUR LIFE: EFT TAPPING USING MATRIX REIMPRINTING

'Abby Wynne reveals a new promise through her book How to Be Well. By creating a steady flow of ideas derived from the human potential movement's major thought streams, Abby takes us to an incandescent awareness. Significantly, she leads us to be the witness of our soul striving for wellbeing, light, evolution, freedom and love. What could be better than these gentle reminders about self-care, lying as gold within the deep seams of our potentially rich love?'

STEWART PEARCE, MASTER OF VOICE, SOUND HEALER AND ANGEL MEDIUM

'Abby has so much to teach us. She stands out as one of the masters of clearing away emotional pain so you can live an authentic, happy and successful life. Her fusion of traditional psychological techniques with New Age spiritual practices makes her process flawless and fool-proof by not just healing your mind but your body and spirit.'

SEAN PATRICK, THAT GUY WHO LOVES THE UNIVERSE

How to
Be Well

How to
Be Well

Use Your Own Natural Resources to Get Well and Stay Well for Life

Abby Wynne

HAY HOUSE

Carlsbad, California • New York City • London • Sydney
Johannesburg • Vancouver • Hong Kong • New Delhi

First published and distributed in the United Kingdom by:
Hay House UK Ltd, Astley House, 33 Notting Hill Gate, London W11 3JQ
Tel: +44 (0)20 3675 2450; Fax: +44 (0)20 3675 2451; www.hayhouse.co.uk

Published and distributed in the United States of America by:
Hay House Inc., PO Box 5100, Carlsbad, CA 92018-5100
Tel: (1) 760 431 7695 or (800) 654 5126
Fax: (1) 760 431 6948 or (800) 650 5115; www.hayhouse.com

Published and distributed in Australia by:
Hay House Australia Ltd, 18/36 Ralph St, Alexandria NSW 2015
Tel: (61) 2 9669 4299; Fax: (61) 2 9669 4144; www.hayhouse.com.au

Published and distributed in the Republic of South Africa by:
Hay House SA (Pty) Ltd, PO Box 990, Witkoppen 2068
info@hayhouse.co.za; www.hayhouse.co.za

Published and distributed in India by:
Hay House Publishers India, Muskaan Complex, Plot No.3, B-2,
Vasant Kunj, New Delhi 110 070
Tel: (91) 11 4176 1620; Fax: (91) 11 4176 1630; www.hayhouse.co.in

Distributed in Canada by:
Raincoast Books, 2440 Viking Way, Richmond, B.C. V6V 1N2
Tel: (1) 604 448 7100; Fax: (1) 604 270 7161; www.raincoast.com

A catalogue record for this book is available from the British Library.

ISBN: 978-1-78180-597-8

Interior images: 22, 48, 56, 91 Alexa Garside/www.brightonillustrators.co.uk

Printed and bound by CPI Group (UK) Ltd, Croydon, CR0 4YY

To the most generous, loving and wise team of beings I have known and shall ever know.

This book is dedicated to you.

don't give up

you can hold the light, even if you feel alone.
those who want it will fly towards it when they are ready,
those who can't take the brightness,
will try to snuff it out.

don't despair

tend to your light, keep it bright and strong.
feed it gently, with love, hope, dreams...
dance in your light, trust it and watch it grow,
expand and know you're not alone.

keep moving towards the light no matter what

there are many lights dancing in darkness,
perhaps unaware of each other
spinning and climbing like stars in the night sky,
over the rugged cliffs and joins in the landscape.

it's time to believe we can make it

what one does makes it easier for others
we are helping each other regardless of geography, geometry,
space and time and all dimensions
knitting together the gaps in our souls

to fill all the spaces with love.

ABBY WYNNE

Contents

List of Exercises,
Meditations and Ceremonies

Chapter 3

Chapter 4

Chapter 5

Chapter 6

Chapter 7

Acknowledgements

I am deeply thankful to the following people for their help, encouragement and the part they played, either knowingly or unknowingly, in the creation of this book: Robert Mohr, Regina Ní Dinn, Cahal Flynn, Michael McKeever, Brian Head, Stephen McCormack, Stephen Brown, Patricia Sheehan, Pamela Miles, Mairead Conlon, Karen Ward and Deirdre Clinch.

My family are my best teachers. In particular I want to thank my dad, Alec Feldman, for his unequivocal support over the years. My love and heartfelt thanks go to Susan Browne-Feldman, Penny Baizer-Botel and Morton Botel, Mark and Brooke Feldman, Estelle Feldman and the Wynne family, particularly Tony and Pat. I also send love and gratitude to my grandparents Elaine and Jack Feldman and Shirley Baizer-Bernstein.

I am so grateful to everyone at Hay House, particularly Amy Kiberd, for believing in me, and my wonderful editor, Lizzie Henry, for taking such care with the script. Big thank you also to Julie Oughton, Tom Cole, Jo Burgess, Ruth Tewkesbury and Michelle Pilley.

I send love, gratitude and admiration to my amazing Facebook community, whose unqualified love and support since the day I opened the doors of my practice have lifted me on wings of appreciation which have kept me going on the days I've wanted to hide away.

My shining stars, my beautiful children Megan, Joshua, Mya and Siân, thank you so much for believing in me, getting excited with me about all my achievements along the way and doing your own thing regardless of how crazy your mama seems to be!

But most of all I want to thank my husband, Ian. Without your friendship, knowledge, wisdom, sense of humour, kindness and generosity, this book most definitely would never have been written.

Introduction

One of the most common problems in the world today is stress. When we are stressed, our body creates the stress hormone cortisol, which helps us stay alert to handle the stress better. Being on red alert for long periods of time, however, makes us ill, and the way we live today we are always on alert, so we are always making too much cortisol.

It would sound simple, logical and straightforward for us to reduce the amount of stress in our lives, which would reduce the amount of cortisol, which would result in our feeling better. Most of the time, though, we aren't even aware of what the cause of our stress is. And because we are constantly in a state of stress, we're often not aware of how stressed we actually are.

Rather than create a book about stress, though, I prefer to talk about *wellness*, where wellness is 'a state of feeling well'. Feeling well means having good mental, physical and spiritual health (yes, spiritual too). When we feel well, we are happier, at peace with the world and have more energy, creativity and motivation. We begin to thrive, and then we strive for things that are good for us, and good for those around us too. Being well means having vibrant health and feeling we deserve good things in life, so we get them. And when something stressful comes along, it no longer happens *to us* because we feel like a victim, it just *happens*, and we bounce back from it more quickly than before because we are able to do so.

Being well can dramatically improve the quality of our life and the lives of our family and the other people around us. It takes work to get well, however; it doesn't just happen because we want it to.

I have created a map to help you move from where you are now to your future healed self. It is all in this book, right here for the taking. The rest is up to you.

So let's look at this book more closely.

About This Book

There are plenty of self-help books out there telling you what you 'should' be doing. I find the theory and the logic behind most of them are good, but they never actually tell you *how* to change your life. I spent years looking through self-help books for the answers and quickly discovered that if I found one answer in each book I was doing well. I wanted to write the book that I was looking for back then. So this book is different. It is not a self-help book. I like to think of it as a self-*care* book. And I include the *how*.

I promise you that in some way, shape or form this book will change your life – *if* you give permission for your life to change. The only thing that's standing between you and being well is you.

So I'm taking the time now to connect with you right from the beginning. The reason why some healing work is life-changing and some is not is to do with trust. I want to get to know you, to talk directly to you, so you can feel that you can trust me and that you have a guide in me. A guide is someone who makes suggestions as to how you can do things in a different or a healthy way for yourself. I know I can guide you to make the changes you need to make to have a life full of joy, health and happiness.

You are the one who has to make these changes, however – let's be clear on that from the start. And if you resist, you might feel that I'm being hard on you from time to time. Now I'm not an advocate of a harsh directive coaching style and I know we may not all be ready to do 100 press-ups or run a marathon. A morning stroll to a café may be all that you can handle right now, and believe me, that's perfectly fine. So right from the outset I want you to take this book at your own pace. Please. If you find you're resisting some of the work, then there's something there for you to learn, and that can't be rushed or ignored. So don't push yourself if you're not ready yet. I'm a great believer in the idea that when you're ready, it's easy. If you're not ready, you can bash your head on the wall to try to get through it, but it just won't happen and you'll end up with a bashed head.

So please put this book down when you feel you need to so you can take the time to digest what you've read. You can't learn these concepts through your mind alone. For them to be truly useful in your life, you need to embody them, and that means experience them and feel them deeply in your body as well as make sense of them in your mind.

A big part of being well is relaxing and accepting who you are. When you do this, you begin to grow or expand.

Over time, you come into balance with the new you, and then you're ready to expand again. This is the way growth works, and you can't rush the process. Imagine that the ideas in this book are seeds that can be planted in a garden – *your* garden. You need to decide if they are the seeds you want and then give them time to grow.

Go gently. Be patient. And take care of yourself. That's how you get well, and stay well for life.

Your Journey of Healing – a Map

Part I: Gaining Awareness

Chapter 1: Who Are You?

We will start by looking at all the different aspects of you, including your physical body, memories, thoughts and emotions. We will discover how you identify yourself (career, family roles, wounding). We will learn about the ego, the soul, life-force energy and energy flow. I will introduce you to the wellness scale and using a journal as a way of tracking your progress.

Chapter 2: How You Connect Energetically Through Relationships

There is a layer of energy we do not see that affects all of our relationships. You will learn about this layer in this chapter and discover how unhealthy relationships impact on your energy. I will give you suggestions on shifting heavy energy to remove the unhealthy effects on you. I will also look at ways of helping you empower yourself by changing your expectations of what a relationship actually is.

Part II: Getting Well

Chapter 3: Healing Your Relationship with Yourself

We start the healing work with ourselves. Here you will learn how to make friends with your physical body and ask it what it needs and wants from you. You will learn how to listen to your body instead of just living from your mind. I will teach you how to be grounded at the energetic level, so you can be empowered and feel stronger. By treating yourself better and hearing your inner voice, you will learn how to be nicer to yourself. This will lead to a greater understanding of what self-care really is and how to do it. And in turn this will lead to an increase in self-worth, self-confidence and self-esteem.

Chapter 4: Healing Your Relationships with Other People

Here I will teach you how to respond in your relationships so that you can set good boundaries. We will look at how you give your power away and I will teach you how to get it back through meditation and exercises at the energetic level. We will then look at basic family systems and how families are affected when someone who is usually sick gets better. I will teach you what power is and how it's different from force, ways of feeling safe standing in your personal power and how to create good boundaries in all your relationships.

Chapter 5: Healing Your Inner Wounds

I liken our energy field to a river: if it runs clear and fast, we're healthy, but most of us are blocked with 'debris' from past wounding. To do deeper work, we must start with a damage assessment. That's where we start in this chapter, then we clear out your river, releasing old wounding and healing aspects of yourself that are hurting. We also look at how you can forgive everyone, even yourself. You will learn why releasing all your secrets is important and how you can bring magic back into your life. This is big work and must be validated, so I also give you some healing ceremonies to honour what you have accomplished here.

Part III: Staying Well

Chapter 6: Maintaining a Good Baseline Wellness Score

All the deep work we have done needs maintenance, so in this chapter we work with the physical body, the emotional body and the mental body to create healthy patterns for vibrant health. We will look at food and emotional eating, exercise and physical pain, rest vs exhaustion, watching what you say and think, and looking at what energies you put into your body. Becoming aware is key, but creating a daily practice of wellness is vital, so we will look at how you can do that too, as well as create a list for emergency self-care when you need it.

Chapter 7: Reaching Your Full Potential

Being well is great, but how can you then step into a happy life? Are you allowed be happy? Here's how to follow your joy. We will look at the three most important things: who you are with, what you do and where you live. I will teach you how to let go of labels and roles and live as your best, healed, self. I will teach the difference between your healed self and your ideal self, and what being human really means. Healing yourself affects those around you too, so we look at healing the space in an argument. And I finish up the book with instructions for creating a life you love using the Law of Attraction. And why not? You've done all the hard work – you deserve it!

Appendix: Choosing the Right Therapist and Therapy

Empowerment is so important and is the emphasis of my work with you. But if done thoroughly, the work in this book will bring up issues that you may not be able to manage on your own. So I've written an appendix section for you outlining the different types of therapy available and how to choose a good practitioner, along with a synopsis of the other things I have to offer and a list of further reading.

PART I

GAINING AWARENESS

*It is only in the gaining of awareness
that we realize what it is that we
already have to work with.*

Chapter 1

Who Are You?

'If you can grow in love, you will grow in awareness.
If you grow in awareness, you will grow in love.'
OSHO

'How can you live without knowing what your spirit
is doing and what your spirit is saying to you?'
CAROLINE MYSS

She looks dishevelled, yet not a hair is out of place. My
client shifts in her chair and touches the side of her face in
a repetitive fashion. She keeps nodding when I ask her if
she's okay. I can see that she isn't.

'You know, sometimes I don't feel that I'm really here,' she
says.

'It's okay,' I say, 'I understand what you mean.'

'You do?' She smiles, sits up straighter in the chair and
looks me in the eye. Something changes in the room, in
her face.

'Yes,' I say, after a minute or two. 'See, it feels as though more of you is here now – am I right?'

'Yes. I feel different now.'

In my private practice I see many people who feel disconnected – from themselves, from their relationships, from life. They are people who suffer panic attacks, depression, melancholia. They are people who feel stuck, trapped or joyless, people who can't stand being around others or being alone, people who are just not happy but don't know how to become happy. Could you be one of these people?

In our lives today we tend to define ourselves by what we do, who our family is or what role we play in our family or in society. Have you ever noticed this when meeting someone new? We say our names, then it's straight into: 'I'm a chartered accountant.' (If we happen to be a chartered accountant, of course.)

I admit it's much easier to answer 'What do you do?' than 'Who are you?' So, instead of tackling this difficult question head on, let's consider who you are *not*.

You Are Not Your Body

You have a physical body. It is made up of your bones, your skin, your muscles, organs and blood. As you grow, you experience life through the senses it offers you: touch, taste, hearing, smell and sight. Your body is the vehicle through which you experience the world. It is also the vehicle through which you express yourself in the world.

Believe me, you know this. When you're in pain, nothing can distract you *from* your physical body. The way you move in the world changes – you may have mood swings, be frustrated, upset and even scared. You may not want to see your friends; you may not go on social outings as often, if at all. Until you are feeling some semblance of hope, or of acceptance and resolution, you're caught in the fragility and pain of your human body.

Look at your body. Think about how you are interacting with it. Take a few minutes to find out exactly where *you* are in it. Are you mostly in your head? Are you connected to your stomach? Are you always aware of your legs and feet? Or do you feel that some of you is slightly outside your head, maybe over to one side? Does this way of thinking seem strange to you?

You might feel as if you are more in your body after a walk, a yoga class or some other physical activity. Do you recognize that feeling?

We are still learning what this tendency to shift around in our body is actually about. Neurologists are doing more and more work on the brain and are coming to a realization that what they thought was an exact science is, in fact, much more complex.

Become aware of your head, your brain in particular, right now as you read this. Now bring your awareness to your feet. Isn't it almost as though you leave your brain for a moment, go into your feet and then come back again? Some people can be in their head and feet at the same time! But having full awareness of the whole of our body is difficult – hearing our heart beat, listening to our breathing and wiggling our toes... all at once! Our brain can only process a certain amount of information at any one time. We do have limitations with this physical body, there's no doubt about it!

Our body changes completely throughout our life. We are born as a baby, develop into a toddler, then transform into a child. As we grow, we have a teenage body, then an adult body, then that of a mid-life adult and eventually that of an elder. Our body is always changing, but the person we are is there, observing the world, learning about it and about ourselves, the whole time.

Sitting at tea between psychotherapy classes, one of my friends was talking about a man she was interested in. She was telling us she was thinking of getting a new hairstyle, in fact a complete make-over, to try to attract him.

There were only three men in my class as psychotherapy is mostly attended by women, and one of them was listening in. When he heard my friend suggest changing her looks, he shook his head.

'When will you ever learn?' he said. 'It's not about your make-up, how much weight you're carrying or the colour of your hair. It's about the person inside *the body. When will women stop worrying about things that are really not that important?'*

You Are Not What You Do

A celebrity chef was on television once and I remember him saying, 'If I couldn't cook anymore, I'd be no one. There would be nothing to live for.' He was so intrinsically defined by what he did that he couldn't imagine himself any other way. Whereas that is an extreme example, we do tend to do this a lot. And if we aren't defining ourselves by our job, the next best thing is to define ourselves by a label.

'I'm depressed. I've done a lot of work on myself over the last 20 years. I've been off medication now for the last two years. I'm back at work and I've just got a spot on the local rugby team.'

'Is it possible then,' I ask, 'that you're no longer depressed?'

'I never thought of that! I suppose it might be...?'

'Who would you be if you weren't depressed?'

'I don't know.'

We also identify ourselves through our role in our immediate family: 'I'm the youngest', 'I'm a mother of four', 'I'm John's wife.'

And we identify with our wounds: 'I'm the child of an alcoholic', 'I'm the one who gets blamed when something goes wrong', 'I'm the peacemaker in the family', 'I'm the sick one' or 'I'm the victim of abuse.'

There are lots of options, but no matter which role we identify with the most, all roles come with limiting beliefs that sink into the subconscious mind and can hold us back. For example, the person who believes they're the one who gets blamed for everything expects to be constantly blamed when things go wrong. If they're *not* blamed for something, as they grow older they start to find ways to blame themselves in order to maintain that identity.

When these roles are taken away from us by circumstances out of our control, we can fall apart. For example:

✻ Someone who has been let go by their firm but identifies themselves strongly with their job can fall into a depression very quickly, as they don't know what they might do instead.

✻ In the case of John's wife, when John leaves, or passes away after 40 years, she no longer knows who she is.

We disempower ourselves when we identify deeply with our role, whatever that role may be, because we become tied down by it and there is no room for growth. Growth happens when we untie ourselves and take the risk to create space.

EXERCISE

Who Are You?

❖ Take a pen and paper and write a list of all the roles you are playing in your life – best friend, cousin, sister, father, etc.

～ Which role is dominant?

～ In which role do you feel most comfortable?

～ Who do you think knows you best?

❖ Start another list on a fresh page and answer the question 'Who are you?' without referring to any of the roles on your first list.

～ How do you feel you did? Was it easy?

~ Reading back over what you've written, do you think it
expresses the true essence of who you are?

✳✳✳✳

Okay, this is a difficult exercise for the first one! But if you
had trouble with the answer, you can see how disconnected
we can become from ourselves, and how caught up in our
roles, the people around us and our own ideas about who
we are.

There is no right or wrong answer to this exercise by
the way, just an opening of your awareness. This might be
the first time that you've seen how many different roles you
play. Were you aware of this? What does it feel like to see it
written down?

> 'I don't know who I am now that I've lost my job,' a
> despondent client says to me.
>
> 'You're still Michael, aren't you?' I ask.
>
> 'Yes, but who is Michael?'
>
> 'I don't know,' I say, 'but won't it be fun to find out?'

The Different Aspects of Yourself

Whatever your roles and labels, you can say that you are the
sum of all the aspects of yourself, where each aspect is a
smaller part of the whole.

Some of these aspects are memories, thoughts and
emotions. There are even parts of you that haven't yet grown
up. You may have heard of inner child work – that's when

you work with an aspect of yourself that is still trying to make sense of something that happened when you were a child. It remained child-like, frozen in time, and can show up in your adult self in the form of anger, frustration or even a temper tantrum. (If you don't think you have temper tantrums, can you think of an adult who does have them? Well, maybe you do too!) I believe that you also have an inner teenager, an inner 20-year-old, and so on. All of these aspects of yourself are looking for the love, care and attention that only you can give to them.

There's nothing wrong with this – it's a natural thing to be composed of many different aspects all thrown together. We are all the sum of the parts of ourselves that rejoice under the sun, the parts that haven't quite grown up, the parts that are hidden, the parts that are angry or grieving, the parts that are here and the parts that have left. Let's look at some of these in more detail.

Memories

Memories are how we remember where we've been, what's happened to us and how we define ourselves. There are two types of memory: long term and short term. Some people think memories are encoded, stored and retrieved entirely in the brain, but there's no exact scientific proof of this. Studies (and anecdotal evidence) do show, however, that when parts of the brain become dysfunctional due to ageing or disease, long-term memories may be more easily accessed than short-term ones. So where do the memories actually reside? And what exactly are they made of?

Memories are stories that are sometimes charged with emotion. They are, admittedly, our version of events. (My father says there are three sides to a story: your side, their side and the truth.) Sometimes we have trouble accessing certain memories; some people don't remember whole chunks of their lives.

Experiencing memory loss due to excessive alcohol consumption is quite common. There is scientific research which shows that if the body has to choose between investing energy in survival and in creating memories, it chooses survival. This explains why so many of us have trouble remembering traumatic events.

I was on the Rolfing table one day for my fourth session. (Rolfing is a form of bodywork that works with connective tissue.) The Rolfer was working on my left leg, moving down towards my calf. Suddenly out of nowhere I had a flash of a memory of a family trip to Euro Disney. We were all laughing and enjoying the experience, even though it was raining heavily.

'Oh!' I exclaimed. 'I just remembered a family holiday I took over eight years ago! I've not thought about that in years!'

'That happens a lot,' the Rolfer said. 'Forgotten memories come to people on this table all the time. It's interesting, as they can be similar memories for different people, depending where on the body I'm working.'

I believe that memories are energies that get tied up in and around the physical body. This means that in order to access them and 'play them back' in our brain, we need to access the energy that holds them. It's almost as if our body is a storage unit or a filing system and our brain is the television screen that we play the memory back on.

Imagine a piano player sitting down on a music stool, putting his hands on a piano and beginning to play a complicated piece of classical music from memory. Where was the memory of the music before his hands knew what to play?

Here's a theory: through an intention in our mind we connect to the energy of the memory we want (the music for example), then that energy releases itself or unwinds from wherever it may be and flows through us to our brain. Then we can remember it.

How can we prove this? Well, maybe we can't, but after years of working with people, I can only say that it makes sense to me. And my clients. And my Rolfer agrees too!

Louise L. Hay's book *You Can Heal Your Life* is all about which parts of the body store which type of emotional energy. For example, she suggests that people who aren't feeling supported store emotional pain in their back, where the muscles can spasm and cause great physical pain. The person may have massages, physiotherapy, hot baths, even painkillers, but the pain never seems to leave them. I believe that the emotional pain comes from the memories they are storing in their back. And it's only when they recognize that pain and work with the memories and beliefs that are associated with it that they get relief. The memories are no longer 'charged' with emotion and the body becomes more peaceful. Then it can heal and the back pain disappears.

Have you ever had a recurring pain in your body that just would not go away no matter what you tried? Do you think you may be storing painful memories there? What could they be about?

Thoughts

Ever find yourself thinking of something when you're with someone and they're thinking of exactly the same thing? Or you both say the same thing at the same time? Do you think that it's possible that you, or they, 'picked up' on the thoughts?

'Thought forms' are energies that are created from thoughts, or it may be that they are created by the thoughts themselves. They may be charged with emotions or not. We don't know which comes first; again, this is not an exact science. Just as I believe memories aren't stored in the brain, perhaps it's possible that thoughts aren't stored there either.

Thought forms come in different vibrations depending on the quality of the thought – happy thoughts are fast and light, sad thoughts heavy and slow, angry thoughts heavy and fast. We tend to think different thoughts depending on how we are feeling, and fearful thoughts can influence how we are feeling and change it dramatically.

Thought forms may be held in our body, but they may also linger in the environment where the thought occurred and be picked up by other people. Some of these thought forms have a long lifespan, so sensitive people may be able to pick up on them long after the people who created them have left.

> *'I was driving my car on the motorway at 10 p.m. on the way home from a night out. I had had a great time, was in a good mood and was nearly home. I was looking forward to a cup of tea and getting into bed when it happened.'*

My client shrinks into his body as he remembers the experience.

'Suddenly, out of nowhere, I felt a huge fear surround me. I started to panic about money. I felt that I had no money. My mind told me that I couldn't pay my bills, but when I thought about it properly, I knew I had money in the bank and I had paid my bills the week before. Yet I still felt the panic around me. I didn't know what had happened or where it had come from. But I knew the panic wasn't mine because it just didn't make sense.'

Thought forms may not affect us in such a dramatic way as in this example, but they can leave reverberations, like ripples in a pond.

❋ 'I walked into the room and felt shivers down my spine. It was creepy – it was as if I could hear voices shouting. Maybe something bad had happened there.'

❋ 'I was walking down the road and suddenly the song "Macarena" came into my head! I'd not heard that one in ages – why did I think of it?'

It can be difficult to tell the difference between a thought form and emotional energy. It's all about how your brain interprets the energy, and your brain can only interpret energies based on your personal life experience. My client and I agreed that the panic he felt in the car was not his and that it was possible that he'd driven into some thought energy that was fear-based. Because it was specifically about paying bills, he'd been able to recognize that it wasn't his fear, even in the midst of panicking. Once we'd worked out how it might have come to be there, he felt better about it. It made sense to him then, and he knew that if it happened again, he'd be better able to cope.

You can see that it's a bit more complex than pure emotional energy and pure thoughts: most thoughts are charged with emotion, just as most memories are. It can be difficult to separate the two.

Here's an example of where I picked up on some specific thought forms. While I was living in Australia, I worked as a data-entry clerk for a classified newspaper. In the beginning, I would go into work happy and I would leave stressed and exhausted. All day the girls who sat in the room with me would grumble and complain about the bosses, about the sales staff, about their working conditions. They felt that we were being watched, and as it was a data-entry job, the computer did calculate how fast and how accurately we were typing, which is like being watched. So the computer logged how often we would take a break and, as we weren't typing then, this included toilet breaks. As a group, the girls started to suspect that we were also being watched in the bathroom. This idea spread to our phones being bugged and our conversations recorded. Over time I had the same thoughts myself. Some days I felt I was being watched at home, in my own house! I had picked up the thought forms of suspicion from these women and was perpetuating them myself. It was not a healthy atmosphere to be in.

Elizabeth Gilbert, in *Big Magic*, describes ideas as 'a disembodied, energetic life-form. They are completely separate from us but capable of interacting with us… they do have a consciousness.' She has some amazing examples of this, including from her own experiences. We are still only learning about thought forms and energies, and there is much to learn.

We'll talk later on about how to work with thought forms. But for now, can you see where thought forms may have affected your own life?

Emotions

We attach emotions to most things to give them a meaning or a value, but what are emotions exactly? We could say that emotions are energies similar to thought forms that we experience though our body, whereas thoughts are experienced through the mind. Thoughts can create emotions, which are then experienced by the body, and the reverse is also true – emotional energy creates thoughts, which are then experienced by the mind.

You can create emotions or you can pick them up from outside yourself and experience them as your own. You can hold on to them, express them or repress them, depending on the situation and your level of personal growth. They are like electricity – they have a 'charge' which can be either pleasant or unpleasant, depending on the situation. When an emotion is attached to a thing, that thing also becomes pleasant or unpleasant to us, depending on what the emotion is.

Just like thought forms, emotional energies vibrate at different speeds. An example of a high and fast emotion would be joy; a low and slow one would be grief. If you feel bright and light in your step and are looking forward to the day, you're experiencing high-vibrational emotional energy. If you're feeling down, depressed or heavy, you're also experiencing emotional energy, just at a much lower vibration. High-vibrational energies tend to dissolve lower ones, so when you're around someone who's laughing, you may feel uplifted and start laughing too. In general we prefer to feel light and fast.

We can recognize emotional energies more quickly than we can recognize thought forms, because they don't come with words. Sadness vibrates at the level of sadness, and our body can recognize sadness because it's experienced it before. It doesn't necessarily recognize whether it's our sadness or somebody else's, however. That's where awareness and experience come in.

We can read emotional energies from other people without having to feel them ourselves. We know if someone is angry, if they're bright and cheery, or if something about them is different (such as when someone has been sad for a long time and suddenly seems happier). Can you relate to the following examples?

- ☘ 'She held out her arms to hug me, but I knew she didn't mean it.'

- ☘ 'He walked through the door and smiled, but I could immediately sense he was angry.'

- ☘ 'There was a sadness there in the background. I could feel it.'

Your Soul

Based on what I have said so far, it seems that you are not your body, you *have* a body. You are not your memories

17

or your thoughts or your emotions, you *experience* these things. So what, indeed, are you?

I believe that you are all of these things combined, glued together perhaps by your soul. So what is a soul?

Just as emotions and thoughts are energies that move at different vibrations, so your soul is also an energy, but it has a consciousness too, a self-awareness. Because it is such a sacred thing, I see it as a divine energy, where 'divine' means 'of God', or 'of Source'. You don't have to believe in God to use the word 'divine', it's just that it's such a special thing that calling it simply 'energy' doesn't do it justice. So choose a different word for it if you feel baggage or heaviness around the word 'divine'.

Your soul is the observer part of you, the part that can see your behaviour in any given situation. It is the part of you that was there when you were a baby, when you were a toddler, the part that has been with you your whole life. I believe that it was there before you were a baby and will be there long after your physical body has died, but you don't need to believe this to do the work in this book. What you do need to know is that your soul strives for health, for light, for personal growth, for freedom and for love.

Your Ego

Your soul comes with an ego, which helps you look after yourself in the physical world (rather than in the energetic world of thoughts, emotions and soul). The ego gets so much bad press, I would like to say upfront that I am a great fan of it. The difference between having an ego and being egotistical is not well understood. We need our ego so we can tell the difference between what is safe for us and what is not. It's our ego that tells us when a saucepan is too hot to touch or that it's really time we went to bed. Our ego is the defender of the boundaries between us and other people. How good it is at doing that depends on our life experiences. It also helps us take care of every aspect of ourselves, and how good we are at doing that depends on how much we value and like ourselves. Being egotistical, on the other hand, is, well, not a nice way to be.

We will look at all of these things later in this book, as I truly believe that wellness comes from working with all the aspects of ourselves and retraining them so they can look after us better. So there's no need to kill off the ego, but we do need to befriend it.

Working with Energies

We are not taught how to work with our energies. To begin with, we have trouble recognizing what is real, what is scientific and what lies outside our own belief systems. We taste, we smell, we touch, we see, we feel; if we experience something that doesn't fall into those categories, out of fear or habit we ignore it, we make fun of it, we run from it, we ridicule it. I cannot tell you how many of my clients begin sessions with me saying, 'You'll probably think this is weird, but…'

Our culture prefers the logical, so we mostly live from our mind, our thoughts. We stop listening to our emotions when we get caught up in life because it is easier, and we depend on our thoughts alone. As I described above, thoughts are only one aspect of who we are, though, so no wonder we often go through life feeling that something is missing. I'm sure you know a few people who feel that way right now and you've probably felt that way yourself at different times in your own life. Truth is, we tend to lose the relationship with what is important, what we have to 'feel into', and we ultimately forget why we are here.

I'm asking you now to take some time out to explore the things you can't experience logically, the things you have to feel; to take some time to embrace the idea that they are aspects of yourself too. I want you to really experience and learn to work with these aspects of yourself in a positive way, so you can empower yourself to be well.

EXERCISE

Exploring the Different Aspects of Yourself

It's time for you to get to know the different aspects of yourself – your thoughts, your emotions, your soul. Are you ready to do this?

Take some time to write in a notebook or a journal how you feel about all of what has been said here. Can you separate yourself out into the different aspects we have discussed – physical body, thoughts, emotions, soul, ego?

Please take all the time you need to do this so that you're clear about all of these aspects of yourself and can recognize them in yourself. It will make it much easier for you once we start to work with them in greater depth.

Here are some questions you can ask yourself:

- What is the difference between experiencing a thought with emotion and a thought with no emotion? Has this ever happened to you? How do you know?

- What does happiness really feel like? When was the last time you felt happy? Do you allow yourself to experience it to its fullest?

- Can you recognize the part of yourself that has been with you throughout your life – the observer part? How do you feel about it?

And some very important questions I want you to really think about:

- How do you feel about the prospect of being well?

- What will change in your life if you become well?

- Are you experiencing resistance to becoming well? Do you fear it? Do you know what this is about?

- Do you have someone who can support you on your journey to wellness? Who is it?

You might not get all of the answers to these questions right away. I find that simply asking them is like planting seeds in a garden – some of them take longer to grow than others. But the answers will come if you genuinely want them to and if you focus your awareness on them. Just asking all of the aspects of yourself to help you with this work can start a chain reaction that will open the way for you to find what you need to help you on your journey to wellness.

Working with Your Energy Body – Your Biofield

The sum of all of your aspects is bigger than your physical body. As I said earlier, emotions and thought forms spill out of you as well as flow through you. Your soul essence doesn't fit into your physical body nice and snugly either, like a pillow in a pillowcase. So there is an active energetic area around your physical body, which is called the biofield or aura. It goes all around your body, above it, too, and down into the ground. It is composed of your emotional energy, thought forms and soul all mixed together, and it fluctuates depending on how you are feeling and how much personal work you have done.

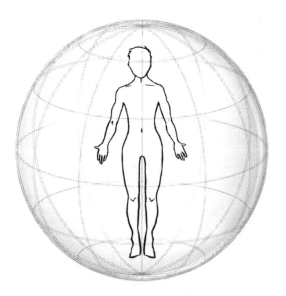

The biofield

Some people have a big, strong energy field, while others are contracted and tight. Although most of us can't see our energy body and it is the part of ourselves that we probably understand the least, it impacts on our behaviour and on our physical world, sometimes in an illogical way, so we can't discount it anymore. It's time to work with it, to become responsible for ourselves and all of the aspects that we are, so that we can learn how to create vibrant health.

'Whenever she comes into the room, I can't help it, I get so angry at her I find myself shouting and screaming at her before she even opens her mouth.'

As she tells me this, my client's hands are clasped around her stomach, as if she is protecting something.

'How big is your energy field today?' I ask her. 'Move your hands outwards and find the edges of your energy, your aura.'

She moves her hands outwards, then back to where they were, close to her body.

'I think it's about here,' she says, almost apologetically.

'Yes, that's where you are today,' I say. 'You're so contracted that when your mother comes into the room you have no space for yourself, no room to manoeuvre. That's why you react to her before she even says anything – you're furiously protecting what energy you have before she takes any more of it from you.'

Our energy body impacts on our physical body, our emotional body and our mental body. So, as in the example above, sometimes we act emotionally without understanding why. We can't make sense of it, but it's usually because there's something going on at the energetic level that needs to be healed.

Our energy body can suffer pain, too. It can be drained and exhausted. Parts of it can leave if we've had a trauma or a shock. It can be inextricably linked to someone who is unhealthy for us and it can be ungrounded and outside us. When pain happens at the energetic level, it can take some time for its impact to trickle down to the mental, emotional and physical levels. But it does. When symptoms appear at the physical level, we treat the physical body, but it doesn't heal completely if the root of the problem isn't dealt with at the level at which it manifested, i.e. the energetic.

Exercise

Discovering Your Energy Body

❖ Take a few minutes to sit down in a quiet space in a chair. If you want to, you can light a candle, dim the lights or play some gentle music, but this isn't required. Do make sure, though, that your phone is off and that you won't be disturbed for five or 10 minutes. Become aware of your breathing.

❖ With flat hands, palms facing inwards, place both hands on your stomach, not overlapping. Move them slowly outwards, creeping millimetre by millimetre until you feel the edge of your energy body, the boundary between yourself and the rest of the world. How do you know when you've reached the edge? It's different for everyone. Some people feel it through temperature or texture, some just know, others see colours. What is it for you?

❖ Reach into your own energy, then reach out of it and see if the feeling is different. When you are in your own energy, how does it feel? What is the texture? The temperature? Can you see your energy? Can you feel a physical change in your body when you move your hands gently in your aura?

❖ How big is your biofield? Does it extend beyond the reach of your fingertips or is it contracted and close to your physical body? It is important to know this, because if your biofield is wide, you have more space around you to respond to events, to respond to other people. If you have a small amount of space around you, you will be more prone to reacting rather than responding.

Don't worry if you can't figure it out now. This may be because it's the first time you've done it or you're preoccupied with something else and not fully focused on the exercise. Ask yourself if what you are preoccupied with is the thought that you're not able to do this. If that's the case, that's okay – it's resistance, that's all. If you relax more into it and give yourself permission to try it, you'll find that your confidence will increase, you'll be more comfortable doing it and it will become easier. Take a break and try again, even over a couple of days, until you feel more connected to what you are doing. You might also find you have more success with this at night-time, when you're more relaxed.

Take a few minutes to write down in a journal what this exercise was like for you. Was it difficult to connect to your energy body? Were you surprised by how contracted/expanded you were? Does that explain some of your behaviour and how you hold yourself in the world? What do you think?

✳✳✳✳

The Wellness Scale

The first step to being well is knowing how you feel right now, rather than just sitting with 'I don't feel well.' When we think *I don't feel well*, we can get caught up in the unwellness of it all and stuck in our complaints, our physical pain, our exhaustion. We then feel miserable and are less likely to want to do something positive to move out of that state. By checking in with ourselves and asking, 'How do I actually feel?' in a disconnected sort of way, without falling into the actual complaints themselves, we get an overall picture of how we are and are more likely to find ways to improve on it.

When you start to check in with yourself it's incredibly useful to have a comparison scale so that you can define where you are in a relative way. For example, knowing you're 5 out of 10 shows immediately that you're not at 1, but you're not at 10 either, so you feel okay – not terrible, but not brilliant. I want you to start using a 'wellness scale' so that you can track how you feel in real time, with a real, measurable value, and really start to see your progress on the journey to wellness.

The wellness scale

I have defined a wellness scale that we will be using regularly in this book. It will be useful for you to keep a note of how you feel based on this scale so you can learn what is making you feel better. Here it is, ranging from 1 to 10, where 1 is where you feel terrible and are low on enthusiasm for life and 10 is where you feel excited and happy with life.

The Wellness Scale	
1	'I feel awful and depressed by life. I don't want to get out of bed.'
2	'I'm very down. I'm up and dressed, but I don't want to be around people.'
3	'I'm quite down and feeling emotional. I'll go out and talk about other things, but not about myself.'
4	'I'm feeling a little bit down. A chat with a friend about what's going on may help.'
5	'I feel okay – not happy, but not sad either.'
6	'I'm a little bit brighter than okay. I can listen to other people's problems and not feel my own stuff too much.'
7	'I'm feeling quite good. I can offer advice to people and laugh and have fun.'
8	'I'm feeling happy today. I'm thinking about doing something fun and making future plans.'
9	'I'm excited and enthusiastic about life. I can cheer others up and I'm doing things I love.'
10	'Life is wonderful! I'm spending time doing things that I love to do and singing and smiling all the time.'

Draw this scale in your notebook. You might like to change the descriptions and put them into your own words so that they feel closer to how *you* feel at the different levels of wellness. Make it your own.

There's one problem with using this scale, however. You can get two readings from it: one from your head, where your brain tells you where you *think* you are on the scale, and the *real* value, the value that your *body* tells you. You need to be aware of the difference between these two values, so that you choose the correct one when you check in with yourself.

EXERCISE

Working with the Wellness Scale

❖ Ask yourself, 'How do I feel right now?' on the scale of 1 to 10 and write down the value in your notebook.

❖ Sitting on a chair with your feet flat on the ground, take a few deep breaths in and out. Imagine that your thoughts are balloons passing by. You're not going to climb into them – just let them pass you by. If you climb into one, you'll drift away from what you're doing here and you'll have an amazing adventure, but you'll lose connection with the work that we're going to do now. If you find you're climbing into a balloon, climb right back out.

❖ Bring your awareness into your body and into the room.

  ~ Start by being aware of the top of your head, your eyes, your cheeks and your mouth. Breathe.

  ~ Be aware of your throat and your chest. Breathe.

  ~ Open your chest and drop into your heart. Breathe.

  ~ Move down into your stomach. Breathe.

  ~ Relax your stomach. Breathe.

  ~ Move into your hips, your pelvis. Breathe.

✦ Now ask yourself, 'How do I feel right now?' on the scale of 1 to 10 and write it beside the first one in your notebook. Is it the same as before? If it is, how long did you spend in your body, breathing and going into it? If it isn't, can you tell the difference between a value that your mind gives you and a value that you receive from your physical body?

It's very important that you can tell the difference between what your mind is telling you and what your body is saying – your emotional body, your energy body. I call this 'feeling into it' rather than 'thinking about it'. If you take your mind's word for something every time, you lose touch with your inner self, your inner wisdom. This work teaches you how to come back to it.

✳✳✳✳

Please don't be upset or worried if you score between 2 and 4 in this exercise. There's work to be done and now you're aware of it. There are lots of things that you can do to bring yourself up to a 5 on the wellness scale and we'll be talking about some of these later on in the book.

If you score a 1, you're more than likely needing some extra support and help to get by, so perhaps you can mention this to whomever you are seeing, such as a psychotherapist/counsellor, doctor or good friend. And if you're not getting help, perhaps you could consider asking for it. There are resources at the end of this book to help you decide who you need to ask. When you're back up at 5 on the wellness scale you can think about helping others, but right now it's your turn to ask for help, your turn to help yourself.

Working with the Wellness Scale

I would like you to check in with your wellness scale frequently during the day. You can get a score when you wake up, and then, as your day progresses, get another score. Check in with the scale in the afternoon and again in the evening. Check in one more time before you go to bed. You'll start to get a picture of your energy levels and how they are affected by what you do during the day.

I often say to clients, 'You can't be available for anyone else if you're below 5.' In order to have something to give to others, you need to have something to give. If you're below 5, you have less energy to spend on other people because you need most of it to keep yourself going. The closer you are to 1, the less energy you have for yourself.

You need energy for life – for enjoyment, for connection, for vibrancy. That's why people get into circles of stagnation at these low levels of wellness. If you want to get more energy in your life, you have to spend energy climbing up the scale to at least a 6, and this can seem a momentous task if you're at level 2 most of the time.

Say you offer to mind the neighbour's children, then go clean your mother's house and go on a hike. If you start the day rating at 4, how do you think you're going to feel at the end of it?

If you're rating yourself as a 2 when you wake up and your needy friend phones you wanting to cry on your shoulder because her boyfriend has left her and she's so miserable and all alone in the world, can you listen and talk to her and hang up feeling better? Or does it drag you down even further? My question to you is this: is it being selfish if you don't pick up the phone to her? My answer is no – it's not selfish, it is self-care. You need to be over 5 on the wellness scale before you can pick up the phone in a situation like that and not feel that you've fallen down further towards 1. And if you don't know where you are on the scale, you don't have a marker by which you can care for yourself. By checking in with yourself, you can see if you're able to pick up the phone, go out to dinner, clean the house or go on a shopping spree without draining your energy.

If you find that you regularly get yourself into the type of situation where you're dreading something and then do it anyway, it's probably because you're a caring type of person or an empath – someone who feels other people's feelings. The dread comes from your energy body, because it knows that you're not in a good state to take more on. Don't worry, this book will help you with strategies for looking after yourself first.

Here is something that might help straightaway: if you really need to pick up the phone, you could say, 'I'm not able to talk right now. I'll call you back when I can.' It's the truth, you know. You're not able, because you're not high enough on the wellness scale. You're not lying – you need to look after yourself first and you don't have to explain why. Learning that you can do this, that it's okay to say 'no' to things, is a big part of looking after yourself. If you're feeling in your heart that you don't have any energy to give to anybody else, you're probably rating between 1 and 4 on the wellness scale and you've nothing to give anyway.

If you're rating a 6 or 7, then picking up the phone will be easier to do. There'll be no feeling of dread or heaviness around it, because you won't be drained down to 0 by it.

You pick up, you talk, you hang up and you still feel above 5 – depending on who it is! You had more energy before you did it, but you still feel better than you would have done if you'd picked up the phone rating at 4. Are you with me? This is what I'm talking about – knowing where you are so you can improve your overall rating; being aware of how you're feeling, so you can look after yourself better.

Finding Your Baseline

Wouldn't it be wonderful if you woke up feeling 8 on the wellness scale? What if you could do that every day? What if that were your baseline?

> *Your baseline is the level on the wellness scale*
> *that you are feeling most of the time.*

Some people have a baseline rating of 3–4. This means that most days they wake up at that rating and they go to work, come home, go to bed and stay pretty much around 3–4 all day. Perhaps something happens at work that brings them down to a 2 or 3, but over time, or a coffee with a friend, they climb back up to 3–4. It's possible that at the weekend they do something fun with friends that brings them up to 7 or 8 for a while, but then when they go home again the level falls back down to 2–3 or 3–4.

The point is that by knowing where you are, you have something to work with, and you can see your progress, so you know what is working for you and what is not.

Your baseline score will improve as you do more work on yourself. It will 'dis-improve' if things around you become difficult and you become overwhelmed. Typically, people who try self-improvement work such as psychotherapy, energy healing or coaching start out with a score around 2–3. After they do some work, their score goes up to 8 because they got something that they really needed. But how long can they hold on to that feeling? Unless they commit to making some positive changes in their lives, over time their wellness score will fall back down to where it was initially. If they do make the changes, their wellness score will fall back too, but it might only fall a little bit, say to a 5. After a few weeks they may find that they are still feeling an overall improvement – maybe maintaining a baseline score of 5. So we can say their overall baseline has shifted from 2 to 5.

Can you see that doing personal work can be incredibly beneficial? Can you see that someone who starts the day with a baseline rating of 5–6 will have a more positive outlook than someone who is at 3–4? What do you think it would it be like to wake up every day scoring 7–8 on the wellness scale? Would you like to find out?

Create an Intention for Wellness

Where would you like to be on the wellness scale every day when you wake up?

I'd like you to create an intention for yourself right now. An intention is an aim, a goal, a plan or a vision that you have for a particular outcome. Deliberately focusing on becoming well through setting an intention invites all of the aspects of you to accept the goal, and then to work together to achieve it.

EXERCISE

Setting Your Intention for Health

Take a few minutes to do this exercise and don't just do it with your *mind*, *feel into* it. Activate your emotional body. Give yourself permission to really step into the images you're about to create.

❖ See yourself waking up in your own bed and feeling happy. Check in with your wellness scale. What are you rating at?

❖ See yourself in the morning going about your day. Check in with your wellness scale. What are you rating at?

❖ See yourself in the afternoon, feeling light and generous with your time. Where are you on the wellness scale?

❖ See yourself in the evening, doing something that is relaxing and calm, enjoying life. Where do you rate on your scale?

❖ See yourself going to bed happy. Where would you like to be on the wellness scale now?

❖ When does this all happen? How soon can you make it real? Imagine a date in the near future when being able to do all of the above feels reasonable to you. Then set a goal using the following template:

> *'On [fill in date] my baseline wellness is [fill in rating]. I wake up at [rating] and I can hold on to that for most of the time.'*

♦ Write this down in your notebook, and remind yourself of it often. If it feels strange to you, redo this exercise until it fits better. It will change as you change, and that's okay!

Finally, remember that feeling well is different from feeling emotional. You can be feeling grief but be light in your sadness. You can be excited about life but calm in your body, not agitated or stirred up.

This is the beginning of your journey to wellness. Accepting where you are now, at the beginning, is so very important. Not pushing yourself too hard and not pretending you're where you're not. Being with the process instead of rushing it. Your journey to wellness starts with you. Are you ready?

Chapter 2

How You Connect Energetically Through Relationships

*'You see persons and things not as
they are but as you are.'*
ANTHONY DE MELLO

*'The best years of your life are the ones in which you
decide your problems are your own. You do not blame
them on your mother, the ecology, or the president.'*
ALBERT ELLIS

Have you found since learning about who you are and doing the exercises in Chapter 1 that something inside you feels different – lighter, happier? You can awaken to your essential self just by giving yourself permission to express yourself fully as a spiritual being in a physical body. Wow! What a gift that can be! But there's more to it than just being yourself: the way that you grow is through your relationships with other people.

Ever spend time with someone and then feel rotten afterwards? Ever wake up sad and not know why? Ever dread the coming week and yet when you think about it logically there's actually nothing that you dread about it? What's going on?

It's a mess out there. Honestly. We're picking up emotional energy all over town, and leaking it out too. We're picking up emotional energy from other people and thinking that it's our own.

Human beings by nature are empathic. This means that we recognize and relate to the emotions that other people are feeling. We do this all the time – we look at someone's face and know if they are happy, sad, surprised, angry... We learn how to do this from a young age. There are even games we can play with children that show pictures with different expressions and the children have to guess the emotion.

If we don't want someone to know how we're feeling, we can become experts in hiding it. We can even hide our feelings from ourselves. (I'll talk more about that in Chapter 5.) But we can't really keep them hidden all the time. Have you ever met someone who seemed happy on the outside and got a feeling that there was something upsetting them? That's our empathic side at work.

Emotional Energy

Emotional Energy Has Its Own Vibration

In the book *Power vs Force*, David Hawkins devised a vibrational scale which he used to classify different emotional frequencies based on research he did over a

20-year period. The slowest, heaviest emotion he classified was shame, which, he said, 'pulls down the whole level of personality'. Imagine how this affects the wellness scale – someone who is experiencing shame falls lower on this scale than someone who is not.

After shame, the next slowest emotion on the list is guilt. Then come apathy, grief, fear, desire, anger, pride, courage, neutrality, willingness, acceptance and reason, then love, joy, peace and enlightenment. The vibration (the speed and motion of the energy) of each of these emotions increases, the higher up the list you go. So, grief is heavy, whereas neutrality is neither heavy nor light.

We have a tendency to say that the slower emotions, such as anger, are 'negative'. But there are no negative emotions, just emotions. And anger can be wonderfully creative if expressed appropriately.

There are no negative emotions –
they are all just emotions.

Instead of working from a scale devised by someone else, perhaps take some time out to see if you can experience grief, neutrality and anger for yourself. Can you call them into the core of your being and feel them, appreciate them and understand what they are? Think about their weight and texture. Contemplate which is heaviest. Can you place them in vibrational order?

Now try the following exercise.

EXERCISE

Experiencing the Vibrations of Emotional Energies

Set aside a few minutes to work on resonating with different emotional vibrations.

❖ Start by coming into your body and becoming aware of your breathing. Reassure yourself that you're only going to work at levels that aren't overwhelming to you – this is just an experiment so that you can see how you 'tune in' to these different emotional vibrations, as if they are radio stations and you are the radio. Take a wellness scale reading before you begin as a benchmark.

❖ Start with a low-vibrational energy such as shame, guilt or grief. Remember a time in your life when you felt this and visualize yourself back there, at that moment, in that place. Remember the clothes you were wearing, the people who were around you, and allow your body to feel the way you were feeling back then. Where does it impact you most? Notice how your body language has changed – are you crossing your arms? Shrinking down in size? Have you dropped a notch on your wellness scale? It's okay – you don't have to stay here for long. Breathe the energy out, come back to the present and feel your feet on the ground. Write down in your notebook how the energy felt in your body.

❖ Now try a higher-vibrational energy, such as happiness, love or freedom. Remember a time when you were laughing with friends or when you felt at peace. Again, visualize yourself there. Bringing the details of the image into your mind can help. Think of the colours, textures…

Where were you? How did you feel? Allow the high-vibrational feelings to trickle into your body and see where they impact you most. What is your breath like now? How open is your heart? Does this feel significantly different from the heavy and low vibrations? Have you moved back up on the wellness scale? Make a note of how you feel and any thoughts that have come to mind during this exercise.

Remember, once you become aware of how your body is impacted by emotional energies, you can work with them to stay higher up on your wellness scale.

Resonating with emotional energies, tuning in and experiencing them, affects your physical body, as you will have seen in this exercise. Low-vibrational energies have the effect of shrinking the body and higher vibrations open up or expand the body. Resonating with particular emotional energies also affects your mind, your thoughts. What do you think happens to your thought patterns when you're exposed to a lower, slower, emotional energy?

Being Sensitive to Emotional Energy

Picking up other people's emotions can be overwhelming if you are sensitive. You might not even realize that you are doing it though, because you may not have been told that it is possible. You do have the ability to shut down, but doing that cuts you off from part of your essential self. When you stop feeling one thing, you stop feeling everything, so aspects of yourself may be suffering because they've been shut down too. And if you haven't shut down but are feeling these vibrations and resonating with them, you may think that they're all yours and there's something wrong with you, or that you have to do work on yourself to get the emotions to shift or move away.

> *'I'm exhausted. I can't do this again.' My client is weeping. Tears are running down her face and into her mouth. She brushes her sleeve across her face.*
>
> *'I don't want to go back there again, not even in my mind.'*
>
> *'What makes you feel that your work isn't done?' I ask her.*
>
> *'I feel so sad all the time. I feel hopeless even. It's exactly how I felt back then. It's how I've been feeling ever since. But I know why it happened. So why am I still feeling sad? Why can't I let go of this?'*
>
> *'What if I were to suggest to you that you* have *let go? That the work we did in this very room together was the work of letting go and that you're done with this piece of work now? What if you're feeling sad because you are feeling sad*ness*? What if it isn't your own sadness you're feeling?'*

Ever heard of ADD? ADHD? Bi-polar disorder? How about autism? Ever wonder why some people who are diagnosed with one of these disorders have trouble going to public places or being around other people?

I've worked with people who are on the edge of these disorders or have been diagnosed with them. One of the main issues they have is that they pick up energies all over the place. Not just emotional energies, but thought forms too. There is so much information flying around in the environment that sensitive people have immense difficulty knowing what is important and what is not. It can be next to impossible to make sense of it, manage themselves in it and protect themselves from it. Some people get completely lost in a sea of information and can't function in the world at all.

You don't have to be diagnosed with or have the symptoms of these disorders to be sensitive to energies. Other signs can be that you get tired frequently, that your body just won't shift weight even when you're trying your best to eat well, that you dread talking to certain people, or you feel heavy or exhausted after being around groups of people or particular people. Maybe you are prone to panic attacks, severe stress or worry; maybe your feelings get hurt very easily or you have headaches often. All these things could indicate you are picking up the emotional energies of other people without knowing it and your body is trying to eliminate them while your brain is trying to make sense of them — no wonder you're tired! Don't worry, there are many exercises and techniques that will help you come into balance, and we'll look at some of them here.

Thinking Differently about Emotional Energies

We need to start thinking in a different way when it comes to emotional energies. What if I were to liken an emotional energy to a perfume? Say you're walking down the street and you suddenly smell the perfume your mother used to wear. What happens to you? You stop, smell it again, and, as you take it in, memories of your mother flood back — moments when she held you tight and you could smell her, moments when perhaps she was away and you sprayed her perfume on yourself to feel her close by. We don't get lost in these memories, as we are aware that we are calling them back to remember something associated with the smell. And they can affect us in a good or bad way, depending on our evaluation of that particular time in our life.

Now apply this idea to emotions. What if you're in the supermarket picking out some food for your dinner and suddenly feel deeply sad? Your immediate reaction will probably be to wonder why. *Oh! I feel sad! What's wrong? What am I sad about? Why do I feel sad? What is this sadness? It reminds me of when my boyfriend left me. But I thought I was over that already. Maybe I'm not over that already. He really did hurt me. Oh dear, I'm sad because he didn't love me. Did he ever love me at all? Maybe I'm completely unlovable...* You can see how we can spiral downwards from here.

What if you were to approach the same scene in a different way? You're at the supermarket picking out some food for your dinner and suddenly feel deeply sad. *Is this my sadness? I don't think I have anything right now to be this sad about. Maybe it's someone else's sadness.* You look around. *Over there, that woman looks upset. She's hunched over, trying to be invisible. Is this her sadness I'm feeling? Oh! It doesn't feel so bad – it's lifting now that I've figured it out. It's not my sadness after all! That poor woman, I wish her peace and love. It's terrible to feel as sad as that.*

Do you see the difference? Same experience, different approach to handling it. Once you know what it is, it becomes like catching a waft of perfume, only now you can recognize it and ask yourself if it belongs to you.

This doesn't mean that every time you're in the supermarket and feel sad it isn't your stuff! You might have a legitimate reason for feeling sad as you decide what to eat, but you'll be aware of that legitimate reason and the sadness will be easier to work with because it's yours, no matter how unpleasant it may feel.

Getting Clear of Other People's Stuff

'Getting clear' in this context means having a clear-out so that you're not carrying 'stuff' around that isn't yours. Cleaning your energy field, so to speak, of emotional energies that you may have picked up, wherever you may have picked them up from. As you begin to focus more on emotional energies and learn how to work with them, it becomes less important to find out what they are all about and more important to discover why you resonate with them in the first place – get it?

'I love my new flat. I have a big room and the kitchen is so much better laid out than in my last flat, yet I get scared in there late at night for no reason that I know of, thinking that someone is going to break in and attack me. I don't understand it!'

My client is shifting in her seat, obviously uncomfortable and distressed.

'Have you ever felt this way before?' I ask.

'No, and nothing has ever happened to me like this before,' she says.

'Who are you living with?' I ask.

45

'A friend that I made recently at work. She was looking for a new place and so was I, so we decided to get one that we could share. Her place had just been broken into at the time and she didn't want to live there anymore – aah, I'm picking up her fear, aren't I? It isn't mine at all. It makes so much more sense now!'

Once she realized what was happening, my client was able to dissolve the fear and feel more comfortable in her new apartment. As she became more comfortable, her flatmate also began to feel more comfortable, because she wasn't picking up the fear that was being reflected back at her from my client.

It's time to get clear!

EXERCISE

Getting Clear of Other People's Energy

❖ Breathe and allow your awareness to come into your body. It's worth spending time getting this right. Do the best that you can and know that as you practise this it will get easier. Here's a way to do it using your breath:

   ∽ Focus your awareness on the top of your head. Breathe. Relax. Rest here for a moment.

   ∽ Drop the focus of your awareness down to your neck. Breathe. Relax. Rest here for a moment.

   ∽ When you're ready, breathe into your chest, relax into it and rest there for a moment.

~ Slowly move the focus of your awareness down your body until you feel more centred there. You can keep going until you're in your legs and feet if you like, depending on how much time you have.

❖ Once you've dropped into your body, check in with the wellness scale and see where you are. Make sure that you aren't listening to your brain telling you how you're feeling, but are going deep inside to check in with your body.

❖ Now say out loud:

> *'Any energy that is not mine, please leave my energy field now.'*

Say it as though you mean it – the strength, confidence and belief that you put into it will be reflected in how you will feel, practically straightaway. If you don't really mean it, nothing will change. So try it again from a deeper place inside yourself and mean it this time. Now wait and see if something shifts or moves away from you.

How do you know the energy has left? You start to feel more relaxed in your body, more settled, more comfortable in yourself. Perhaps you were holding yourself tight somewhere and that seems to be a bit softer now. Maybe your breathing has changed or you're not feeling as emotional.

❖ Say it again:

> *'Any energy that is not mine, please leave my energy field now.'*

And again wait. Perhaps you feel a softening in the back of your neck this time, or a muscular release down your arms or legs, or a relaxing of your stomach...

* Check in with the wellness scale and write down the new value you're feeling.

* Did you notice a big change? Write down any thoughts you have around that.

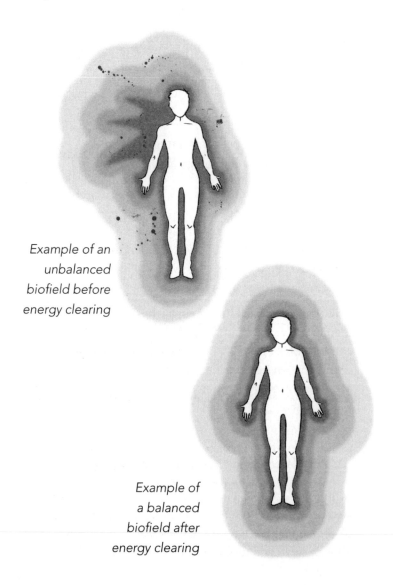

Example of an unbalanced biofield before energy clearing

Example of a balanced biofield after energy clearing

Being Responsible

Part of the work we are going to do here is not only noticing what other people are doing to us but also becoming aware of what we are doing to other people. That's the responsible part.

If you've just completed the 'Getting Clear' exercise, you can combine it with the next exercise in order to have a clearing technique in which you're taking complete responsibility.

EXERCISE

Calling Your Own Energies Back

Just as you pick up energies from other people, so you also leave energies out there that others can pick up. It's time to call them back.

❖ Check in with your wellness scale before you begin.

❖ When you're ready, drop into your body as before, mindfully, and relax into it, with your feet flat on the ground.

❖ When you feel fully present, say out loud, with the same conviction as before:

> *'Any energies that are mine and with other people, please come back now.'*

You can change this to something that resonates better with you if you like, such as 'I call back any emotional energies I may have released, knowingly or unknowingly, that are with anyone else' or words to that effect. It's all in the intention, which is to release your emotional energies from other people's energy fields.

❖ Now wait. What do you feel? Many people feel more whole. You may think that the emotional energies you released were unwanted and if you take them back you'll feel bad, but when you do call them back, it often feels as though a part of you that was missing has come home again.

❖ Take some time out to write about this in your notebook. And don't forget to take a wellness scale reading, just to see your progress.

Relationships Are Complicated

'I know I broke up with him over four months ago, but I can't stop thinking about him. It doesn't make any sense. He doesn't call me, I don't call him, it was a very clean break-up and we both agreed it was for the best. But every morning when I wake up he's the first thing I think about and every night I can't get him out of my head.'

My client starts to cry. She is visibly in emotional pain.

'I need to move on from this,' she says pleadingly.

The people we care about the most are the people we are most deeply connected to, whether through romantic relationships, friendships or family ties. These energetic connections may be more complicated than simply 'dumping' emotional energy on someone else. By releasing people from your emotional energy and freeing yourself from theirs, you will really start to notice a difference in your energy, and in the relationship too, and it's always for the better.

> *'I feel a sense of dread when my sister comes to visit. I know that things are difficult for her at the moment and I really want to be there for her, but I feel so tired after she visits me, most times I can't do anything else for several hours afterwards. Last time I went to bed straight after she left. It was only 7 p.m. I love her dearly, but right now I can't spend time with her. I don't like feeling this way – I feel I'm being selfish.'*

If you'd like to experience life to the full, you need to start by disconnecting yourself from other people's emotions, thought forms or unhealthy connections to you. This is a big step, but a very healing one, and one that could change your life for the better, and quite quickly too. Try the exercise above with people you're in relationship with who are causing you difficulty and see what changes for you.

Remember that when you can tell the difference between who you are and who you are not, and when you can see and accept all the parts of yourself, you're taking steps towards being able to express yourself fully and freely here in this physical body in this lifetime. When that happens, you experience joy, peace, happiness and lightness right now, in the present moment. What could be better than that?

Emotional Energies Get Stuck in Space and Time

In the next exercise we will work with your memories of a particular incident that upset you. I will show you how you can remove the charge of emotional energy around the memory so that it doesn't upset you as much. Choose a memory that isn't greatly upsetting to start with. You might want to come back to this exercise again once you know how it works, so you can go deeper with it.

EXERCISE

Calling Your Energies Back from Specific Moments in Time

❖ Take a few minutes to remember a time where you felt tired, drained or ill after spending time with someone else. Don't be judgemental – they wouldn't have done this on purpose. If you find this difficult to believe, you might need to write down all the reasons why you are angry/ upset at them, then you can breathe it all out of your body and relax. Try to believe that it really wasn't them doing something to you, it was just something that happened.

❖ Think about how you felt at the time and how you feel now, knowing that you may have taken on someone else's emotional energies. What would it be like for you to be able to clear these without feeling them yourself?

❖ You can use your intention to clear energies that you've picked up from someone else and to call back your own energies that they may have picked up in return. To do this, you can close your eyes, check in with your wellness scale, then breathe, drop down into your body as far as you are able and relax. Breathe, drop down, relax. Breathe, drop down, relax...

❖ When you feel you are deep in your body, visualize the place and time where this event happened. Visualize the other person. Remember as much detail as you can, as if an artist is erasing the room around you and painting back in that actual scene just after it happened. Breathe again and feel the ground beneath your feet.

❖ Now say:

*'Any energy that is not mine, please
leave my energy field now.'*

❖ Wait and see if you are actually holding on to it. Notice if your body tenses up or if it relaxes even more. You might need to reassure yourself that you are safe.

❖ Visualize your energy field opening up, give yourself permission to relax and say it again:

*'Any energy that is not mine, please
leave my energy field now.'*

❖ When you feel that you have let go from your shoulders and neck, from your chest and stomach, from the back of your heart and from your lower back, breathe and relax even more deeply.

❖ Now say:

*'Any energies that are mine and are with other
people, I welcome you back to me right now.'*

❖ Breathe and stay with this for a few minutes to allow the energies to return.

❖ When you feel ready, bring your awareness to wherever you are, stretch and move and feel your body in the here and now. Allow the scene around you to dissolve and come back into the room you are sitting in.

❖ Now check in to your wellness scale. Notice if you have shifted up or down. Write down any thoughts in your notebook.

❖ If you want to do it again, ask your intuition if there is anyone else or any other memory that you need to repeat this exercise with. Wait for an answer from your body, your spiritual inner wisdom. And then do it. Part of this work is making the commitment to do it. So, if something is beginning to open up for you, stay with it and go deeper with it. But always check in with yourself afterwards to make sure you are feeling centred in your body and okay to go on with your daily activities.

You may find that doing this exercise once has great effects on your physical body and you notice deep changes almost right away, but when you go about your daily activities, energies can 'sneak back' in or out when you're not looking. So you may find that you have to repeat the exercise every day for a week, for two weeks, even for a month, depending on what the relationship is and whom it is with.

As well as calling her energies back from her boyfriend in a general way, my client and I used this exercise with her memory of the day she broke up with her boyfriend. She then thought of some other incidents that had taken place with him that had upset her, and we carried out the exercise for them too.

'After we did the energy exercise with my ex-boyfriend in session, I still woke up the next day thinking of him, but I did it again myself a few times over the next few days and it gradually became more bearable. After a week or two, I stopped thinking about him altogether. I feel freer now. Thank you for teaching me that technique. Now I can move on with my life, finally!'

Why do we need to do this exercise more than once? There are many reasons for this – the main one is that some aspects of us are unwilling to give up all the energy in one go. In the case of my client whose relationship broke up, part of her refused to believe that the relationship was really over and wanted to hold on to some of her ex-boyfriend's energies for as long as it could. Her mind knew it was over, but this small part of her didn't want it to be over. As she continued to do the exercise with persistence and patience, that part learned to trust that it was actually okay to let him go. Finally, she was able to release all of his energy and move on with her life.

Sometimes clearing the energies between you and someone else is the best thing that can happen in your relationship, as it frees both of you up to be yourselves in a clearer way.

'I felt guilty doing that exercise with you around my sister. I felt that I was being selfish or something disconnecting from her. I even felt a little scared of doing it. But afterwards I felt great. And it was amazing – just after our session my phone rang and it was her! She sounded brighter, happier even. I tried the exercise myself again the day after, and the day

after that. Afterwards I stopped dreading my sister's phone calls and I was able to invite her over for dinner last night. It feels so much better between us now and I even think she is feeling better too.'

Energy Ties

Not only do we leave bits and pieces of our energy lying around in buildings or with friends or family, we can also become energetically tied to people. Energy ties are different from the type of connections we've spoken about up to now: ties are active things that are alive and flowing between our energy field and someone else's. These ties, or cords, establish themselves when the subconscious gives permission for them to be formed. In other words, we don't know we're making the connection in our brain; some other part of us agrees to it.

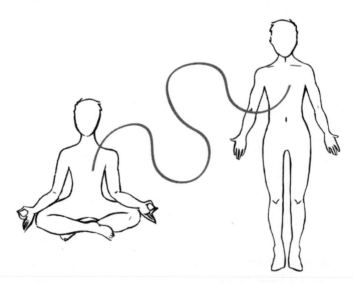

Example of how two people may be connected by an energetic cord

As babies, we connect energetically with our parents, more usually with our mother, because we need our parents to survive. The urgency that we feel around survival as a baby leads us to create direct energy bonds between our energy field and our parents' energy field so we never feel separated from them. This fundamental relationship between parent and child forms the basis of all the deep relationships that we enter into in our lifetime. Just as we attach energetically to our parents through energy cords, so we tend to connect to sisters and brothers, friends and lovers in a similar way.

Even in the healthiest of relationships, I believe that energy cords can drain both people involved and block them from expressing their essential selves. But they can be cut and healed.

Sounds harsh, doesn't it? Just sit with the idea for now and I'll share some examples and reasons why I believe that these cords must be cut on a regular basis.

Experiencing Energy Ties

When someone close to you is worried about you, they can be thinking about you all the time, but there is often more going on energetically. The energetic cords between you can feel like a 'pull' or a pressure, and can affect everything, even though you might not be aware of it.

'I don't feel comfortable here,' says my client, squirming in her chair. 'I don't mean here with you, I mean in Ireland. It's as though there is something missing, something not quite right.'

Sabina is from Poland and has been living in Ireland for two years. She has just been offered a three-year contract worth a lot of money and she isn't sure why she is thinking of not accepting it.

'I want to stop being so upset. I love this job and it is a great opportunity for me, but I spend nights crying and I don't know why. I don't want to go back home, but it feels as though I'm not allowed to stay here.'

'Take a few minutes to come into your body and breathe,' I say to her. 'Is there someone or something that's pulling you away from here, maybe someone in Poland who is missing you?'

She catches her breath. 'My mother. She doesn't want me to stay here, I can feel it. She says she is happy for me, but I can hear otherwise in her voice. I know she isn't telling the truth.'

It's not that Sabina's mother is doing this on purpose – it's not intentional – but energetically there could be an aspect of Sabina that still wants to please her mother and an aspect of Sabina's mother that is still treating Sabina like a child. The resulting energetic connection can feel like a stranglehold for both Sabina, who feels trapped in her life, and Sabina's mother, who is caught in a perpetual state of worry.

Once Sabina realized that it was her mother's worry causing her distress, we did some energy clearing and loosening of the energy ties rather than cutting them. Sabina then phoned home and reassured her mother that she was happy and had the offer of a good job doing something that she loved.

As the ties became even looser, her mother was able to see Sabina's point of view for the first time. She came to visit *her and saw how well she was looking after herself and they even had some fun together. We were able to cut the ties then. Sabina's mother gave her her blessing and Sabina felt much more settled in Ireland after that.*

You can see from this example how loosening and then cutting energy ties can free both people up to grow and expand and feel better. And when it's done this way, gradually over time, the cords are less likely to reconnect subconsciously.

Imagine that you are connected to someone and they are not feeling well, perhaps waking up every day at 1 or 2 on the wellness scale. Let's say it's your sister. When she starts her day, she thinks she isn't well and then touches in with you, whom she thinks of as being well and capable of managing life. By doing this, she inadvertently tunes in to the energetic ties she has to you and starts to pull energy from you.

Remember this is all done subconsciously, not deliberately. You wake up the same day, starting off at a 6 or a 7 on the wellness scale. In the shower, an image of your sister flashes through your mind and you start to feel upset and wonder how she is doing. At the very same time, your sister receives energy from you and starts to feel well enough to get out of bed. However, now you feel drained and aren't sure why. As you move through the day you recover your energy levels, but every time your sister pops into your head (which is several times), you say to yourself, 'My poor sister, I hope things turn out better for her. I wish there was something I could do to help her.' And all the while you are feeding her energetically and facilitating an unhealthy energetic relationship.

This can go on for years, and if you don't understand the energetics behind it, the relationship dynamics won't change.

Cutting Energy Ties

Cutting ties can be scary, because we become used to them and actually depend on them at the subconscious level. We can feel closer to the person we are connected to through that gentle tug that we feel when they call on us, and we need to learn that it is safe not to connect to them that way. I didn't cut Sabina and her mother's ties straightaway, because I knew that they would reconnect to each other almost immediately. Cutting ties is like a leap into the unknown. Can we look after ourselves if we are no longer connected to someone we care for?

I once had a friend who was in physical pain for most of the time. I cared about him a lot and I knew that we were connected energetically. One weekend I was at an energy medicine workshop and the teacher told me that unless I cut the tie with him, I couldn't do the work we were going to do in class.

I was surprised that the teacher was able to see what was going on. And I knew then that, difficult as it was for me, I really had to cut the tie. I struggled with it for a long time, though. Then, just before the coffee break, around 11 a.m., I focused my attention on where I thought the tie was. I visualized my friend in my mind's eye and said, 'I am so sorry, but I have to close this energetic connection with you today. I need to learn and grow and I cannot do that while you are still connected to me like this. I hope you'll be okay and that you understand.'

When I did this, I felt so much energy come back to me so quickly I shot forwards as though I had been hit on the back by a football. I was shocked! And then I felt great. And then I felt guilty for feeling great! And then I felt a little bit angry about the whole thing. And then I let it go – no point in dwelling on it, there was a class to attend.

I didn't say anything to anyone, but my teacher looked at me and nodded and I knew the job was done.

That evening on my way home from the class, I got a text message from my friend. This is what he said, word for word: 'Had an amazing day, got a breakthrough around 11 a.m. and I've been writing, laughing and enjoying life ever since. Best day in ages. Hope you're having a great day too.'

Wow. The risk paid off. I admit, part of me was disappointed – if I'd been feeding him so much energy and he was doing so much better without me, maybe I'd been holding him back the whole time!

Hearing how well he was doing without being connected to me was a big lesson for me. We both gained a lot from the experience and it also helped me realize that we don't do healing, we simply create a space for it to happen by itself.

So, how do you cut energy ties? Most of the time, disconnecting from someone at the energetic level is so simple you won't believe it. The key to it working completely however, is to give your full permission for it to happen. You might be ready to do it and you might not be. So, before you try the following exercise, ask yourself if you're really ready, and if you feel nervous or anxious, you might want to spend some time with that feeling and go deeper into what might be holding you back.

And if you need some extra motivation to do this, know that whether you know it or not, people who are connected to your energy influence the thoughts and decisions that you make. It's so important to be clear and free of all relationship cords so you can be whole and independent of others. You are here to be completely yourself, to bring your light and creativity into the world as yourself. When you cut energy ties, it creates a space for healing to happen all around you. It raises your energetic vibration and you feel lighter, clearer and more present for your life.

Exercise

Cutting Energy Ties in a Relationship

❖ Take a few minutes to think of a relationship that you would like to work with today. It doesn't have to be the most important relationship in your life right now, but it does need to be one that has an impact on you, one that you can use to learn how to trust the technique, so you can come back later and do it again on a different relationship.

❖ Breathe, come into your body, relax.

❖ Visualize the person you want to cut cords with in your mind and connect to how you feel about doing that. Maybe you'd like to take a wellness reading. If you're anxious, check in with yourself to see if you're really ready to do this. If not, that's okay, don't push yourself too hard. If you know for the most part that this is important and you're mostly ready to do it, then know that no harm will come from it and that both you and the other person will benefit from this exercise.

❖ Visualize the energy ties between you and the other person. Notice where they are in your body, where they are in theirs. Take the first image that comes to your mind, rather than trying to make logical sense of it. Breathe into it, relax and know that it is okay.

❖ To cut the ties between you and the other person you can say the following out loud, in a confident voice:

'I ask for any energy ties between me and [insert name] to be cut for the highest good of all concerned.'

'For the highest good' means that you, the other person and anyone else connected to both of you will be better off because of this shift in the relationship.

❖ See how you feel once you have said it. If you feel no change, you might like to say: 'I give my full permission for the ties to be cut between me and [name] for the highest good of all.' And mean what you say, too.

❖ Give it a good five minutes sitting with this to allow the energy shift to take place. It could take longer to clear all the energies between you and the person you have chosen to work on, but now you have started the process.

❖ Check in with your wellness scale and see if the number has shifted.

If you are feeling any anxiety around doing this exercise, ask yourself what the anxiety is about. And don't do the exercise quickly and then rush into something else – make some time to sit and really notice how you feel before and after you try it. And yes, you may need to create some space for yourself to do this, as it is more powerful when you say the words out loud.

If you're still not happy about this exercise, perhaps in your visualization of the ties between you and the other person you could shrink them down a bit, so instead of being big pipes between you they could be small straws or thin tubes. See how that feels. Or maybe you need to work on the permission part and find out what part of yourself isn't happy about doing this.

Perhaps you need a few days to shrink the cords, as Sabina did, before you can cut them completely. Just make sure you check on them and repeat the exercise frequently until you are able to cut them completely, or at least feel a substantial shift in the energy dynamics of the relationship.

You may notice the difference between the times you ask to cut ties with your full permission and the times you don't fully give permission. You're asking all the aspects of yourself to allow you to cut the ties. When one or more aspect doesn't give you its permission, it's probably because it doesn't feel safe to do it, or it needs something from you before it is able to do it. This is where you might need to visit a professional to do deeper work on your inner wounds. We will look more at that in chapters 4 and 5.

You're asking the aspects of the other person to release you too. These aspects can hear you, even if the other person's brain isn't hearing you directly. So the person might have a dream about you, or they might feel that you've disappeared from their life or have moved 1,000 miles away from them, even if you only live around the corner.

You'd be surprised how connected we are to each other. As I keep saying, there's much more to us than meets the eye. We also have what I call 'helpful energies', energies with consciousness that surround us and act as guides or gatekeepers throughout our lives. You could call them power animals, fairies, angels or spirit guides if you want to, or you could just feel safe in the knowledge that there are other energies, at different vibrations, that can help with your healing journey if you let them. We will look at how they can do this in some later exercises.

Social Media Creates Energy Ties

We are spending much more time on social media than ever before. Are we aware exactly what the impact of all of this connecting to people is actually doing to us on the energetic level? Stop and think for a minute. Are you on social media? How much of your time do you invest in it? Why do you keep going back there? What is the draw?

What might be interesting is, say for Facebook, to think of who pops up on your newsfeed the most frequently. Does a Facebook friend you don't know in real life pop into your mind out of context on a regular basis? What I've found is that friendships made on Facebook with people you've never met in person can be just as energetic a connection as traditional friendships. And if you choose to Skype those people, or send them a direct message such as a text or an email, it's as if the energetic ties between you have more places (or dimensions) in which to form.

Social media is for the most part fun and good, yes, but it's also important to be aware of all of your energy connections when doing the work of cutting ties, so that you leave no stone unturned.

EXERCISE

Cutting Ties from Relationships on Social Media

❖ Come into your body in a safe space and breathe. Close your eyes and ask yourself, 'Who on social media is connected to me through energetic ties?' As you sit there, allow people's names or faces or the avatars or images they use to portray themselves to come into your mind's eye. Take your pen and paper and write down everyone who has come up for you.

❖ How many people are there? How does it feel to see this list? Are you surprised?

❖ Check each name. Who feels 'heavy' to you, feels as though they are pulling on your energy – your chest, your heart, your stomach, even your lower back? What would it be like for you to disconnect from them? Ask yourself how that would feel. Do you need to have this relationship at all? What would it be like for you to block this person from you so that you don't have to interact with them anymore? Or do you just need to be more mindful when it comes to them?

❖ Sometimes you have to take physical action to clear energies that are connected through cyberspace. Unlike face-to-face relationships, it's easy to delete, unfriend or block people we don't really know well who have latched onto our energy field in some way. Depending on the social media platform, you may be able to simply unfollow them.

❖ Remember, if you don't take positive action, things will stay the same. If it feels clear and good in your physical body to block/unfriend/unfollow a person, then listen to your body and do it.

❖ Once you have the list of people from whom you need to disconnect, you can use the previous exercise to do just that. If you don't know what a person looks like, that's okay, just imagine a physical body to represent them, or imagine their profile picture or their avatar.

❖ Take your time with this. Do it as often as you feel you need to. And then notice how you feel afterwards. Check your wellness scale. Notice how you feel the next time you see that person in your newsfeed. Perhaps this time you don't feel the need to make a comment or respond to what they are saying. You might also notice a shift in the frequency you see them in your newsfeed too!

The amount of energy that moves in or out of your energy field as you do this type of work depends on how much you mean what you say, how deeply connected you are to a person and the nature of the relationship. If you don't really believe that saying the lines I gave you will make a difference and you've been saying them half-heartedly, then maybe you've felt something shift, but it's more than likely you haven't. If you are closed off to the work and to the ideas in this book, then they won't work for you. That's okay, you might not be ready for them yet. But if you really do want to try the tie-cutting exercises again, ask for the ties to be cut from a stronger and more confident place in yourself. That will make a difference.

In any event, you'll need to repeat the exercises a few times before you feel fully safe giving up all of the energy connections between you and the people you have chosen. I would recommend starting with one relationship and trying the exercise once a day over a few days. When you don't feel a change or a shift anymore when you do the exercise, then you are probably clear of that connection – for now, anyway. Then you can work on another relationship.

If you feel called to work on several relationships at once, it could be that they are all connected to each other. That's okay too. Work with your inner wisdom. You know yourself and your situation better than I do!

Remember, when we have an affinity with someone, the cords can reconnect over time, so it's useful to check in from time to time and ask that they be cut and healed again. In this case, 'affinity' doesn't necessarily mean that we like a person, it just means that whatever the dynamics of the relationship are, they are directly related to our life lessons and are something that we will keep reliving until we learn better.

Cutting Ties Raises Your Vibration

When you successfully cut ties, your energy chemistry changes and you vibrate at a different rate, usually a much higher one than before, as the weight of the pull between you and the other person is released. You may find that the people who pulled on you when you were at a lower vibration aren't able to pull on you anymore.

When you give of yourself energetically, you give your energy away. There will be times where you may feel you have nothing left to give. By cutting ties you are closing off one way that people drain you, and indeed, one way that you drain other people too. Feeding energetically off people is not the way to help them. Trust this. Once we stop doing it, we open up to the more natural higher-quality energy source that is available to us and we can move forward with life.

Keep track of where you are with this work. Trust your inner voice and your wisdom. If you feel that you are still connected to certain people or they have reconnected to you, cut the ties again. Do it and be so aware of your ability to do it that if someone comes back to reconnect to you, you'll notice it straight away and say a big energetic 'No!'

You're getting your power back. You're clearing your energy. Well done!

PART II

GETTING WELL

*Letting go of heavy emotional pain
and reorganizing how we see and
interact with the world lead to intrinsic
growth and a sense of wellbeing.*

Chapter 3

Healing Your Relationship with Yourself

'Low self-esteem is like driving through life with your hand-brake on.'
MAXWELL MALTZ

'The only person who can pull me down is myself, and I'm not going to let myself pull me down anymore.'
C. JOYBELL C.

If you've done the exercises so far, you'll be feeling much better already. By clearing the energy from other people that was caught in your energy field, reclaiming your own energy and disconnecting from unhealthy energy ties, you'll have brought your energy field into a much healthier state. If you haven't, don't worry, you may need some more time with the exercises in the previous chapter. This is *your* process, so go at your own pace.

Where do you go next? How can you start feeling even better than you do now?

This chapter is split into two parts. The first works with how your physical body feels, the second looks at how you feel about yourself. When you bring both of these things together, you heal your relationship with yourself.

In Gratitude for the Physical

Let's face it, in our culture today our idea of how well our body serves us is based on how it looks more than how we feel inside it. Are we too fat? Too thin? Does our belly stick out? Are our hips too big/too small?

Everywhere we look, somebody's idea of beauty is being thrust upon us. We forget what true beauty is because we're always being *told* what it is. Things are changing now, thankfully, and more and more people are awakening to the fact that beauty on the outside is just one part and that beauty is also on the inside. More of us are realizing that every aspect of us is striving for light, for growth, for joy. Isn't *that* beautiful?

If you're not fully awake to this just yet, perhaps give yourself permission to change your ideas around what beauty actually is and let it trickle into your life until you recognize that there is so much beauty in you, too. If we could see the beauty of our divine energetic aspect, really, truly see it, and see it in other people too, how could we ever hurt anyone?

However in the three-dimensional world, many of us are more concerned with our clothes, make-up, skin colour, hairstyle, jewellery and shoes. These are all superficial things that can change over time, but we get too attached to them and disconnect from our actual body and from our essential self.

Our body is the central point through which we process emotions and thoughts. 'Process' means we experience them, work through them, clear them and let them go. This can be uncomfortable when the emotion is grief, anxiety or pain, so we tend to disconnect from our body to avoid the feelings we don't like. But when we're disconnected, we can't feel pleasant emotions like happiness either. It can be difficult to reconnect to our body if we've been away from it for a while, but we do have to reconnect if we want to be well.

'What can I do for you?' I ask a new client.

'Well,' he says, 'I was holding my baby, it was his first birthday party and everyone was so happy, singing and blowing out the candle, and I felt that I wasn't really there. I know that work is taking a lot of my attention, but when I was standing there surrounded by my family, I knew that this wasn't right. I was looking at my family and they all seemed so happy and I felt nothing. I don't want to live my life like this.'

Here I suggest a very gentle exercise: treating your body like an old friend you haven't seen in a long while. All you're going to do is say to your body, 'Hello, I see you. Thank you for all the hard work you're doing for me.'

You can do this exercise in segments over a period of time if it becomes overwhelming. Ideally, take some time to really go deeply into it. If you feel anxious just thinking about doing it, take out your journal, do a wellness scale check-in and then ask yourself why you feel anxious. What's going on for you? What's coming up? Remember, wherever you are with yourself is where you're supposed to be at this very moment in time. See this gentle exercise as something that can really help you reconnect with your body and release quite a substantial amount of the stress that you may be carrying.

EXERCISE

'In Gratitude for My Body...'

The beauty of this exercise is that you can go as deeply into it as you feel comfortable. You can be fully clothed and do it in your head wherever you're reading this book (even in public!), or you can do it at home in bed, or in the bath, speaking out loud – it's completely up to you! You can spend time with the body parts you're appreciating by looking and touching them as you speak to them.

See your body as part of yourself that you want to treat a little bit better, rather than seeing it as your whole self. Your body *is* part of yourself. Feel grateful that you have a body. Try to connect to the feeling 'I'm so grateful to be here right now, in whatever shape I'm in at this present moment.'

And now:

❖ Close your eyes for a moment and get in touch with your essential self. Bring your awareness more into your body.

❖ Imagine that you are stepping out of your body and turning to face yourself so you can see your body as a whole, maybe for the first time. Your body is truly doing its best with what you've been doing with it, with whatever you've experienced in your life. Look at the stretch marks, the scars, the colour of your skin. Remember all the things that you and your body have been through together – that's practically everything. Breathe in and out and feel your body breathe in and out with you. Give yourself permission to come back into it. Allow yourself to get a sense of how it's feeling. Say 'hello' to it.

❖ Now go to specific body parts and say 'hello' and 'thank you' to them. I like to start with the feet and work my way up. As you get familiar with this, you can start with the head and work your way down, or just go to those parts of your body that you feel need attention.

You can stop here if you like and come back later and go further with this. See how you feel.

If you are disabled or parts of your body aren't fully functioning, don't worry, you can still do this exercise. You still need to appreciate these parts of yourself, even though you may feel they aren't serving you the way you would like them to. Believe me, it's good to be friends with all the parts of your body, then they make better friends with you and start to serve you better.

I feel this 'getting to know you' exercise is vital for the rest of the work we are going to do, so, difficult as it may be for you now, know that each time you try it, with a fully open heart, you will get more comfortable doing it. Try the following, and feel free to replace my suggestions below with your own dialogue – it's *your* body, after all.

❖ Starting at your toes, bring your attention there. Get into your toes, wiggle them, feel as though you are in them. Say to them, 'Thank you! Thank you, toes, for being there to support me, to help me keep my balance. Without you, I know that I wouldn't be able to walk forwards or stand stable in my life.'

✦ Imagine what it would like to be your toes. Think of all the shoes that you've squashed them into, all the miles that you've walked together, everything you have been through together. What do they need from you right now?

✦ Listen to them, don't make up an answer from your brain. They might say something like 'We need to breathe. Can we walk barefoot for a while?' or 'We need some attention – we'd love a good soak in a bath of Epsom salts' or 'We deserve to look pretty – we want a pedicure!' They may even say, 'There's something wrong; we need you to go see the doctor and sort it out.' Write it down if you think you won't remember. Tell your toes that you'll look after them and give them what they need, and make a date to do whatever it is that they've asked of you, if anything.

✦ Breathe with your toes. Come into balance with them (this means that everything between you has been said, you're not hiding or denying anything they've asked of you and they feel happy that they've been seen and heard by you) and say 'thank you' again.

✦ Then come back to your body as a whole. Breathe. Relax.

✦ Now it's time for the feet. 'Thank you, feet, for being there for me, for connecting me to the ground...' Think of a few other things that your feet have done for you in the past. What have you done to them that you might like to apologize to them for? Do it!

✦ Ask and listen to your feet. What would they like from you? Make a commitment to do it, just as you did for your toes. Write it down if you have to.

- Then move away from your feet, come back to your body as a whole and breathe.

- Do this for your whole body, working your way up from your feet to the top of your head. Spend time in every part of your body, in appreciation of all the hard work it is doing to keep you alive.

- Check your wellness scale once you have done it. See how much higher up you have moved.

This may seem like a lot of work and, depending on how long it's been, your body may have a lot to tell you! So break it up over a few sessions.

You don't have to start with your toes. If your stomach needs the most attention, start there.

Begin to see your body differently. Start to appreciate it in the condition that it's in, instead of seeing the bits that don't match up to the condition you wish you were in.

Make friends with your body – remember it's doing its best with what you are giving it and is reflecting back to you how you feel most of the time. Together you can change anything.

You might want to talk to someone about this exercise – about how it made you feel. It might help to write this down in your journal.

Once you make friends with your body, you're more likely to be comfortable in it and then you'll want to treat yourself better.

This exercise is centring: it brings your energy field more fully into the centre of your physical body. This can be an emotional experience and you may find yourself crying or getting angry. Just breathe through the emotions. Know that you have been holding on to them and now they are unwinding from your body and you're processing and releasing them.

> 'You are more in your body now. What does it feel like?' I ask my client.
>
> 'Tight,' he says, 'stiff and tight, especially around my chest. I think I need to go back to the gym!'
>
> He laughs.
>
> 'Yes,' I say, 'disconnecting from your body allows you to avoid the aches and pains to a certain extent, as well as the difficult emotions. But, as you've experienced, it cuts you off from the beautiful ones too.'

If this is the first time you've felt you've been in your body in a long while, I recommend you try this exercise every day for a few days to settle into it before continuing on with the rest of the work in this book. Get used to this as a new way of being, as a baseline.

Being centred in your body is a great place to be when you have to make decisions, think clearly or be present for other people. See if you can commit to focusing your awareness more on your body every day and connecting it to the highest vibration of energy we have access to: gratitude. It's so worthwhile taking your time with this to get the full benefits.

Grounding Your Energy in Your Physical Body

Grounding happens when you connect your energy field to the ground. The difference between being centred and being centred and grounded is only clear when you have experienced them both. I have had clients who are experts in yoga and teachers of meditation and say they're grounded, but after being taken through a grounding exercise, they feel the difference.

It's difficult to describe being fully in your body, stable on your legs so you're not going to fall over. You stand taller and feel solid, more present, real. You're aware of your body and how you are feeling. You are in balance.

This next exercise is a grounding exercise. You may have trouble doing it the first few times, particularly if you haven't tried the exercise above. But don't worry – practice makes perfect. Just commit to having a go maybe once a day for a few days in a row. You will notice the difference once you put the work in.

Checking in with Yourself

Before you start, check in with yourself. Register how you are feeling on your wellness scale and make sure it is a body reading, not one from your brain! I can't say it enough: getting into the habit of checking in with yourself many times a day really helps you get to know where you are, what you need and when you may need to do something more to keep yourself feeling well.

Hopefully you have noticed an improved score as you have been moving through the exercises and writing things down in your notebook. If, however, you're moving down on the scale, go back to some of the earlier exercises and try them again before continuing with this next stage. It's possible that something in your life has changed or something has happened since you last checked in that is causing you stress. You might even be slowly releasing something connected with your healing process. Don't worry, don't get caught up in it, just give it as much time as you need. As you let go of the heaviness and stress you're carrying, you'll improve your baseline wellness score and then you'll be better able to bounce back from new stressful situations. They are what they are. Life will always have challenges for us, and accepting that takes the pressure off.

And when you're ready, you can try the next exercise.

EXERCISE

Grounding: Part I

Energy flows through your body like water in a river. As you do the work in this book, you become aware of the state of this river (i.e. yourself), its ebbs and flows, its blockages, its straight runs and its turns. If your river has twists and turns, the flow is a lot more clogged and caught up in itself than if your river is straight and strong. So before you start this exercise, open up your body as much as you can by uncrossing your arms and legs, softening your shoulders and making sure that you are comfortable, not wincing from pain or contracting from discomfort.

I have written this exercise with the intention that you can do it while you are holding this book in your hand and reading it. It can be difficult to really ground yourself, as I've said before, so I don't expect that you'll be able to remember all the details of this exercise and then do it from memory. So, while you are in your open position, hold your hands loosely across your stomach and have the book in as comfortable a position as possible so that you aren't straining your shoulders, arms, or indeed your eyes.

You will be working at a deeper level than with the gratitude exercise. You are going to where your body holds on to emotion, which is why you need to go gently with it, at your own pace. That way you can build up trust and learn how to relax with yourself.

Your body stores up emotional energy, so when you come to a spot in the body that feels blocked and stops you from moving on, you can actually ask that part of the body what the problem is. By listening with an open heart, you may hear a message that will help you solve an issue, heal physical pain or give you an answer to something that's been troubling you.

These messages come not as fully developed sentences, but as images, or flashes of thought or memory. Our soul has no spoken language – images and sensations are its ways of communicating. So you might catch a smell, or hear a sound, or see/feel/hear words in your mind. A message might come up as an emotion – you may want to cry. That's all okay. Imagine that by doing this work you've tapped into a cloud of emotion trapped in your body and by crying/breathing it out, you're allowing it to leave and your body to heal. Don't get caught up in it, don't try to make sense of it or figure out the why or wherefore. Don't look for the story in it. Just be with the energy of it and allow it leave your body and free you up for joy.

✦ Start by bringing your awareness to your body and your breath, to the words you are reading right here and now. Place your two feet flat on the ground. If you're wearing high heels or thick-soled shoes, you might feel better removing your shoes altogether. Do it now if you need to!

✦ Imagine that all of your energy is gathered in a big ball of light sitting at the top of your head. Wait for the shift in your energy field as it reorganizes itself to match. Feel this happening and notice how you feel in your body. (Remember, the more you do it, the more sensitive your physical body will become to these energy shifts.) If you can't feel your energy, imagine you have a butterfly net and you're catching all of it in big sweeping curls of the net and pulling it down into a ball at the top of your head.

✦ With your focus locked on to this beautiful ball of light, which is now touching the top of your head, become aware of your breathing. Feel your breath going in and out. Open and soften your chest. Take three soft, deep breaths in and out. And again. And once more. With each breath, release any resistance you may be feeling to this exercise. Soften your body and open it. It becomes so much easier then.

✦ Now you've connected to your breath, you're going to use it to do some work for you. When you're breathing out, use your imagination and your intention to visualize the ball of light dropping down into your body. The amount this ball will drop down with each breath will depend on different factors, such as if your energy flow is open and clear (like the rushing river) or if there is a lot of resistance (like a twisty river with lots of blockages). Know that there is no wrong or right here – it's all good and it's all okay. Accepting where you are allows your body to open, allows the blocks to shift and allows the energy to flow.

✦ So, connecting to the ball of light and connecting to your breathing, allow the ball of light to drop down behind your eyes. Take as long as you need to get there, and when you do, check in with yourself and notice what you feel. You may not be able to put words to it. That's okay. Just make a note that something has changed and notice how it feels to you.

✦ When you're ready, focus, breathe and imagine your ball of light is dropping down again, this time into your mouth. It's funny how you suddenly become more aware of the inside of your mouth when you do this – the backs of your teeth and how your tongue feels! You might realize that you were clenching your jaw, so you may want to stretch your jaw and release and soften your jaw muscles. Stay with your mouth for the moment and just breathe in, breathe out, and be with your mouth, your jaw, your tongue, your teeth.

✦ When you're ready, drop the light down into your throat. Notice if your throat is tight or soft. If the muscles are tight or under stress, they might have a message for you. You can ask your throat if everything is okay. Breathe in, breathe out, stay with the throat and neck. Do you need to hear a message from your throat? Is there something your body needs to tell you that you have been ignoring? If not, that's okay. Let your throat answer these questions, and listen with your heart, not your brain. Just by being aware of your throat, you are making a connection with the energy there, and that may be all you need.

- Focus again on your breath, on the ball of light in your throat. With the next breath out, drop down into your shoulders. Your shoulders bear the weight of the world on them. Notice if you are holding stress there and see if you can use your breath to soften and release the tension. If you want to, ask your shoulders, 'How can I ease things for you?' Stay with the shoulders and wait. If no messages come, it might be that you need to build up trust with your body and try the exercise again in a day or two.

- Focus again on the ball of light, on your breathing. Now bring your awareness to your chest and allow the ball of light to drop down into your heart centre, at your breastbone. Some people feel very uncomfortable here as their heart is trying to tell them something they don't want to hear. If it's the case for you, stick with this exercise and do as much as you are able. We'll work with the heart later, and as you begin to clear the issues blocking it, it will allow you to come into it more deeply. If you're afraid of doing this, it's okay too. Work with the fear, not against it. You can do it! Imagine that with each out-breath you're breathing the fear out of your body. Wait here and do this as long as you need to until you come back into balance.

Just getting to the heart centre can be enough for some people, and that's okay. It's hard work doing this when you're not used to it and you might really feel that you want to take a break from the exercise. Go stretch, check your emails and then come back to finish it off, or try again tomorrow and see if you get a little bit further with it.

The bad news is, however, that you can't take a break at this point, go wash the dishes and make a cup of tea and start back where you left off. You have to start right back at the beginning at the top of your head. However, the good news is, it won't take as long for you to drop down to where you left off. It's almost as though you've cut a path through a forest so you can get there more quickly. If you do leave it a day or two before you try again, the forest path could become overgrown. But the more you walk through the forest, the more defined the path becomes, and the deeper you go into your physical body. It does get easier.

EXERCISE

Grounding: Part II

❖ Focus in on wherever your attention is right now and breathe yourself from your head right down into your heart again. Don't rush this – it isn't about doing it quickly, it's about doing it *deeply*. Check you are fully present. Notice if your heart feels more open, or perhaps a bit lighter, and the ball of light that is the very essence of you is brighter and shining fully.

❖ Now bring yourself back to your breath. As you breathe out, allow that beautiful ball of light to drop down past your heart centre and into your stomach, just above your belly button. Does it feel tight or soft? Try and relax a little bit more, breathing in softness and breathing out tightness.

❖ As you breathe in and out, invite the ball of light, your awareness, to come fully into your stomach and allow it to settle, so you can really get in touch with how you are feeling there.

❖ Drop down again to your navel, and then drop down to just below your navel. How does that feel? Your stomach is your centre of strength and self-confidence in the same way that your heart is your centre of love. So if your stomach is unsettled, you have digestion problems or suffer from nervous anxiety, it could be related to issues around self-confidence, self-image and feelings of personal power. Notice how your stomach feels. Ask it what it needs from you today.

❖ Focus on your breath, and when you're ready, imagine that your ball of light drops down to your pelvis and then splits into two equal parts, one for each hip. Stay there a moment, allowing your hips to come into balance, left and right.

❖ As you breathe, move the balls of light down each leg, equally and slowly. Imagine that the muscles and bones in your legs are opening up, that the channels in your legs are clearing with every breath, with every movement of your awareness. Are you in balance? Is your awareness more in one leg than the other? Can you shift it so that you are in both equally?

❖ Move your awareness into your knees and behind the knees, and just stay inside your knees for a moment. Imagine that they are opening up, both front and back, making more space for the energy to come in more deeply. Move your awareness down past your knees into your calves now, opening up the muscles in them as you breathe out and feel the energy flowing through your legs.

❖ Spread your feet out now on the floor and imagine they are opening up so that they can contain all of this beautiful energy. Become aware of the bones in your feet and visualize the balls of energy entering your feet, making a connection with the Earth. Your energy may be pooling up at your feet, but don't worry, it isn't going anywhere. You're fully in your body now, as much as you can be at this time. And the connection you are making now is going to anchor you, to keep you grounded, stable and strong.

✦ Now for the Earth connection. Imagine you're dropping a cord of light from each foot into the floor. It can go through anything – the floor covering, the foundations of the building you're in… You can take it down 15 floors if you need to. Travel down in your mind's eye with your energy cords through the steel and the foundations of whatever building you are in. Travel through the ground, the rock and stone. Keep going until you can imagine or sense the big, heavy, thick roots of strong old trees, buried deep, deep in the soil, beneath the rocks. Imagine you are wrapping your cords of light around these tree roots. Feel that you have created a very strong connection there.

✦ Breathe now and relax. Slowly bring your awareness back up to your feet, back to the room you are in. You may feel a bit clearer, more connected to the Earth.

✦ Relax now and gently breathe out any emotional energy that came up in your body as you connected through your cords to the Earth. Do this as many times as you need to. Visualize yourself letting go of heaviness, anxiety, anger, fear, guilt and shame – anything you no longer want to hold on to. You're safe now.

✦ Come into balance with how you're feeling. It's time for a wellness check-in. On a scale of 1–10, how relaxed do you feel? How calm? How balanced? Do you feel more at peace than before you started? Wouldn't it be great to stay this way all the time?

❖ When I have clients reach this point in the grounding process, they feel completely still. Some say that they feel heavy in their body, as if it's the first time they have been fully present. One of my clients said her feet felt fat. Because she'd never really been in her body before, she didn't know what it felt like to be in her feet!

This *is* a lot of work, but so worth it. Next time you try this exercise (yes, you have to do it more than once!), put the book aside and see if you can do it on your own. If you've done this exercise slowly, you'll really have noticed the difference, but if you've done it quickly and not spent enough time at each body part, you may not be grounded at all.

This exercise can be done daily as part of a spiritual practice or it could be something you do on a regular basis to help you disconnect from everything around you and come back to yourself again. Start to accept that if this really helped you feel better, it is work that you'll need to factor into your everyday life for the rest of your life.

If you don't really feel any change at all after trying this exercise several times, don't worry. Maybe there's something your body needs you to do before it will relax enough to let you in. You could be afraid to let go of emotion you've been holding on to for years. Start asking the questions and trust that the answers will come. Maybe you'd like to write in a journal about how you're feeling.

Grounding Tips

If you're sitting cross-legged on the floor, you can ground yourself directly by imagining you're dropping cords directly from the base of your spine into the floor. If you're sitting in a chair, you can ground yourself through your legs to your feet and then through the floor. If you're in a tall building, up several floors, you can ground yourself by imagining your cords of light are moving all the way down however many floors are beneath you and then through the concrete foundations of the building right into the ground. See what works best for you.

Grounding through the base of the spine

Grounding through the legs and feet

If you're in difficulty, upset or grieving, you may be overwhelmed by emotion, so grounding in a slow, dedicated way as we've just done may feel too difficult. That's okay. Lying face down on the floor can really help. When you feel the connection between your heart and the floor, you can connect to the Earth directly from your heart and imagine a trapdoor opening in your heart, then dump the grief directly into the ground (and close the trapdoor again before you get up). Your imagination is instruction for the aspects of yourself without language. By imagining things deliberately, you are in essence giving permission to those aspects to heal themselves.

'But I Still Don't Feel Any Difference!'

Some people who try this grounding work just can't bring their full awareness all the way down to the ground. If you can't, that's okay. Don't worry. Perhaps there's a medical/mechanical/emotional issue your body is trying to protect you from. If you've tried and you've not been able to reach your feet, perhaps that's the most you can do today. It's probably more than you've done before, so try again tomorrow. You might find doing this exercise outside with the support of nature can help, especially if you're surrounded by strong trees which are deeply rooted and grounded. You may go a bit deeper tomorrow than today, depending on how much you trust the process. Every day you may go a little bit further as you grow into this new way of being. That's the nature of a journey.

Everybody has the capacity to get there, but how *you* get there is personal. I had a client who couldn't feel any difference when she did her grounding practice, but after a time she noticed that she was more confident in her approach to life. When things were going well for her, she let her grounding practice slide (as you do) and her confidence went back to the way it had been before. So she realized the two things were connected – being grounded and being confident. Even though she didn't feel any difference when she did her grounding practice, it did make a difference to her life. Be open to your life changing for the better in different ways when you work at the energetic level with your body.

Needing Some Extra Help?

This book may not be enough to give you all of the support you need as you release emotional energies. Do you still feel overwhelmed? Are you still stuck getting into your body? Take some time and figure out whom you could talk to about it. Is there a good friend or relative available? If not, maybe you could consider consulting a psychotherapist or a spiritual healer, or having some massage or bodywork to help get the energies moving and enable you to release the emotional pain you've been holding on to for so long. Look at the resources at the back of the book (*see page 245*) to learn about the different types of therapies available and how to find a good practitioner. Don't wait – if your body says, 'Do it,' then it's time to do it.

In Gratitude for the Rest of You

We've looked at coming into your body, being centred and grounding yourself. Now we will look in more detail at how you feel about yourself and I'll give you some techniques you can use to raise your vibration and feel better.

How Much Do You Think You're Worth?

Not that you can put a price on yourself for a market stall, but I'm asking you, do you value yourself enough? Do you invest the time you need to look after yourself or aren't you worth the effort? Do you encourage and support yourself? Or do you call yourself names, tear yourself down, tell yourself you're not good enough and never will be able to achieve your goals?

Wouldn't it be wonderful if you had a best friend who loved you and wanted what was best for you above all else? How about changing the relationship you have with yourself so that you become your own best friend? So that you can learn how to value yourself more? Do you know what happens when we do this? We blossom.

Getting It Straight in Your Mind

If you put yourself last because you feel you don't deserve whatever it is you need, you don't get what you need, end of story. Like my client who neglected her grounding practice and lost her confidence. Ten minutes a day was all it took for her to feel empowered in all aspects of her life, yet because she didn't feel she was worth it, she let the practice slide. Self-care means looking after yourself better, giving yourself more so you have *more* to give. It's not being selfish – being selfish is putting your desires above other people's needs.

Let's define some important concepts:

Need: Something essential that is
required for your health/wellbeing.

Want: A desire for something that isn't necessary
for health or wellbeing but is nice to have.

Self-care: Looking after yourself, ensuring
your needs are met and that you are well.

Selfish: Wanting significantly more than you need
and placing your desires above other people's needs.

Sometimes we think we need something when we just want it. Sometimes we actually need something and we don't give it to ourselves because we think it is being selfish. Can you tell the difference in your own life? This is something you may need to spend some time thinking about. It's okay to have wants, by the way – there's nothing wrong with that, as long as your needs are met first.

As someone who works in service to others, I need to give myself a high level of self-care so that I am always at my best and can offer my best self to people. If I were to neglect my own self-care while helping others, I would burn out in a short period of time and have nothing left to give. I see myself as a model for my clients. When they see me at my best, they hand me their trust and set about their work with enthusiasm, because they see that they can be like that too.

What about you? Do you give yourself what you need?

'When I come home from work, I'm exhausted. I cook dinner for my mum, then I sit in front of the TV for the night eating snacks. Crisps, chocolate, wine – anything I can get my hands on. I wish I could stop doing this.'

My client is frustrated. She knows she needs to eat better and cut down on snack food, but she just can't seem to sort it out for herself.

'What types of things do you cook for your mum?' I ask.

'Oh, anything she wants – pasta, meat and potatoes, salad, curry, you name it.'

'And do you eat with her?'

'Oh no, I never eat with her. In fact, most of the time I skip dinner.'

'What do you do for fun?'

'Fun? Nothing. I don't have time for fun,' she says. 'I'm much too busy.'

By making dinner for her mother, my client is looking after her mother's needs, but by not eating dinner too, she isn't looking after her own. She is filling her need for pleasure by eating snack food instead of making a regular time to do something fun for herself. It's time to recognize that pleasure is a need as well, and if we deliberately make time for fun, we can have a more balanced lifestyle.

In order to make time for fun, however, we have to feel that we deserve to have it, and most of the time the problem is that we don't value ourselves enough to do that.

Some more definitions:

Self-confidence is belief in ourselves and our abilities.

Self-esteem is how much we like ourselves.

Self-worth is how much we value ourselves.

If you have low self-worth, you will automatically have low self-esteem and low self-confidence. Self-confidence can be worked on – you can gain new skills, you can learn by experience – but if you don't value yourself enough, you won't put the time in. And if you don't value yourself enough, it's very difficult for you to find something about yourself that you like.

The work I want you to do here is aimed at increasing your self-worth. Once you start to value yourself more, everything changes.

We will start with looking at repetitive thought patterns and how you talk to yourself. If you don't value yourself, you'll be constantly putting yourself down, talking yourself out of things, telling yourself that you're not good enough. It can take a long time to recognize what you are doing to yourself, or you can catch it right away if you're ready to. Don't judge yourself while you do this work. You are where you are right now and that's okay.

Exercise

Journaling Your Inner Voice

Carry a small notebook around with you for a week. Yes, a week! Focus on how you treat yourself, how your inner voice talks to you. When you catch yourself thinking something like *I could never do that* or *That was a stupid thing to do*, write it down. It may take a while for you to even catch yourself doing that; when you do, don't judge it, do it without emotion. Collect these thoughts together each day, and at the end of the week, create a time and space to read back over what you've said to yourself.

How harsh are you being to yourself? Would your best friend say those things to you? And most of all, is everything really true? Are you as bad as you tell yourself you are? Can you really not do or achieve things? Don't you deserve better?

By spending some time looking at what you are saying, you are becoming more aware of what could be a hidden aspect of yourself.

How do you feel now that you have more awareness of how you talk to yourself? Are you surprised when you see it in writing? It makes it all the more real, doesn't it? It can be upsetting, too, to see it there in black and white. But you can transform it.

Using the Wellness Scale to Transform Your Self-Worth

You're going to call on all of the aspects of yourself now to help with this part of the work. You will need your body, mind and soul in agreement that this is something worth doing. So, before you start this exercise, take a few minutes to check in with your wellness scale, get a reading and ask yourself, 'Is it safe to increase my feelings of self-worth?' Stop and breathe and notice how you feel. If you're nervous about it, stop and work with that before you go any further. Breathe out the nervousness. Go back and do the grounding exercise again. You don't need to be in a rush to do this work, honestly you don't. Reassure yourself that you will be okay. Then try this exercise – but only if you feel safe doing it.

EXERCISE

Using Energy Healing to Increase Your Self-Worth

You're used to using the wellness scale now. How about transforming it into a self-worth scale?

❖ Take a moment to come into balance with the idea of doing this. Take your time. Now, where do you rate on the self-worth scale right now, at this moment? No judgement, remember it is what it is. And it will get better, so be honest with yourself, let go of your mind and 'feel into' what it is. Did it change when you did that? Let the rating shift and change until you get a true reflection of your self-worth. And breathe. It's going to be okay.

❖ Imagine that your feelings of self-worth are represented by a closed box. Can you visualize it in your mind's eye? What does it look like? Like a pirate's chest? Or is it plain? What is it made of? What shape is it? What colour? Allow your subconscious mind, your soul, to reveal an image to you that truly reflects what you feel your self-worth looks like. Connect to this image, no matter how dusty, dirty, rusty or vibrant this box may seem to you.

❖ Now say, 'I give myself permission to increase my feelings of self-worth.' What does that feel like? Do you feel anxiety around it? If so, go and do the grounding exercise, breathe out the anxiety, and then come back here and try this again.

❖ Imagine that there are riches beyond your wildest dreams in this box, ones that you didn't realize were there. Allow the image to shift and change to reflect this increase in value. Focus your awareness on the box of treasure and feel it growing and increasing in its vibration, and at the same time see the rating on the scale increasing to match it. So you're multi-tasking. Say your self-worth rating starts out at 4 and you have a dusty pirate's treasure box as your image. See the box becoming brighter, as if it's been dusted off and got a new coat of varnish, and the rating shifting up to a 5. Can you push this further? See the pirate's treasure box being painted with an ornate design, while your self-worth rating goes up to a 6. How do you feel when you do this? Uncomfortable? Or 'Oh yes, this is the way it should be'?

How far can you take it up the scale? Transforming a dusty old pirate's box into an ornate gold-plated treasure chest with diamonds studded around it can take a long time, but it can be done.

How did this exercise feel to you? Difficult? Probably! It even feels difficult to me at times. We're not used to targeting our self-worth so deliberately, or giving ourselves permission to feel more valuable. Know that when you come back and try this exercise again, you may have shifted back down a lot – or a little bit. It is what it is. Know that the more you value yourself inside and out, the more you will stabilize at the higher levels.

Who do you value the most in your life? Think about it. Are they worth more than you are? Why? Why are you so special that you are worth less than anybody else?

Truly allowing yourself to feel just as valuable and important as anyone else isn't the same as logically *knowing* you are. We're not logical beings, we're multi-dimensional, there are many aspects to us, and in order to increase our self-worth, all of those aspects have to be on board. So, when you try the exercise to increase your self-worth, you could really feel the shift but not be able to hold on to the changes for very long. It's not that your soul doesn't want to, it's that your ego, your mind and your thought patterns still need to shift to a higher vibration to match. So keep doing this exercise, and then, when it feels more comfortable to you, complement it with the exercise below.

Taking Your Thought Patterns Up to a Higher Vibration

From 'I can't' to 'I can' is quite a big leap. If you don't truly believe you can do something but you tell yourself you can anyway, you create a gap, and you can fall into the gap from time to time and get stuck there. So don't lie to yourself. If you don't believe you can do it, whatever the 'it' is, be clear in yourself that it is a self-*confidence* issue, not a self-*worth* issue. And if you need help, decide that you will invest in yourself to either get the help you need or to upskill yourself.

Here are some affirmations to help you with this part of the work. An affirmation is a powerful statement that, when said with conviction, acts like a tuning fork for your vibration. Your body, mind and soul shift to match its vibration if you give permission for that to happen.

The key is to mean what you say when you say it, 100 per cent. Anything that's less than 90 per cent true for you is not as powerful. So choose an affirmation that's slightly higher in vibration than you are, but not drastically higher, so that you don't create a massive gap. Once you settle and relax with it, you will embody its vibration. Then you can choose another one to take you higher again.

I have placed these affirmations in order from lowest to highest. Say them out loud and notice if you feel them 100 per cent. For example, do you believe 100 per cent that you don't need to create emotional pain for yourself? If not, start by giving yourself permission to stop creating emotional pain for yourself.

* 'I do not need to cause myself emotional pain.'

* 'There is enough pain out there in the world. I will no longer create pain for myself.'

* 'I no longer need to hold myself back by creating pain for myself.'

* 'I am learning how to be nicer to myself.'

❋ 'I give myself permission to be nicer to myself.'

These are about feeling well/happy:

❋ 'If a stranger outside on the street deserves to be happy, I also deserve to be happy.'

❋ 'I am a valid human being and I deserve to be happy.'

❋ 'I deserve to be happy.'

❋ 'I want to feel better.'

❋ 'I give myself permission to feel better.'

❋ 'I am allowed to be happy.'

And these relate to self-esteem:

❋ 'I am a human being and I am allowed to make mistakes.'

❋ 'I accept myself just as I am.'

❋ 'I accept myself completely as I am.'

❋ 'I am good enough just as I am.'

❋ 'It is good to be me.'

❋ 'I like being myself.'

❋ 'I am happy being myself.'

Which one of these affirmations reflects where you are now? If none of them do, can you write one for yourself? There has to be at least one in each list that you can believe 100 per cent or you wouldn't be reading this book.

You can take one from each list if you want or start with the first list and work your way through that. Use your wellness scale as you do this (multi-tasking again): get a wellness reading, then say the affirmation, breathe, imagine yourself moving up the wellness scale, sit there a while, then see if you can say the next affirmation … and so on!

There will be parts of you that aren't happy with this work, aspects of you that will want to sabotage what you're doing. That's normal and natural. We'll do some work with those in Chapter 6. But if you need some help now, don't hesitate to see a counsellor, a psychotherapist, a life coach or a healer, or talk to a friend you trust. It's part of the process to resist the work. You might even want to just walk away from it for a while and take a break. That's okay too. Know it's there waiting for you when you're ready.

Know, too, that even a small increase in your self-worth can bring big positive changes into your life. When your self-worth improves, you stop treating yourself so badly and say 'yes' to the things you want. You stop thinking you're not worthwhile and spend time investing in yourself, having fun and doing the things that you love. Your wellness baseline scale shifts to a higher level.

The downside is that the people around you won't recognize you anymore. You will be different. We will work with the implications of this in the following chapter. But for now, just enjoy who you are becoming.

Chapter 4

Healing Your Relationships with Other People

'Everything that irritates us about others can lead us to an understanding of ourselves.'
C.G. Jung

'If you think you're enlightened, go spend a week with your family.'
Ram Dass

As we begin this chapter, take the opportunity to spend some time with your wellness scale and see how you are feeling. I encourage you to check in with your wellness scale every day when you get up in the morning. You can use the reading you get to help you plan your self-care for the day. For example, if you are 5 or below, consider committing to doing something that day that will help you feel better, or perhaps cancel something that may drain you too much. If you have planned lunch with a friend who is high-maintenance, imagine not going to lunch and see if your body feels better. If it does, cancel lunch. You can say something like 'I'm not able to meet you today. Can we make it another day?'

If you're not able to cancel the thing that's taking the most energy from you (such as a business meeting or a job interview), then look at what else you have lined up for the day and factor in some time for yourself. You can then practise some of the exercises from this book so that you free up some of your energy and manage it better.

Right now, you're probably feeling calmer, more peaceful and more empowered than you did before. Why not start to bring your new awareness and these new skills and tools into your day as a regular practice? This will help you to get the best results.

In this chapter we will look at how to create healthy boundaries with other people, so that you stay clear energetically and feel better for longer. Remember, if you're going to work on a relationship, the other person will feel the effects too. You need to be prepared for that shift in dynamics. Go slowly with this, particularly if the person is someone you care about, so that you grow into the new boundaries gently rather than shock either yourself or the other person.

Taking Back Your Power in Relationships

I believe that there is an aspect of our essential self that is our source, or resource, of power and strength. When we need to be strong, we draw from this resource, and if it is depleted or low, we don't have very much power available to us. When we're feeling powerless, we also feel worthless or as if we have failed; these feelings create disempowering thoughts which then hold us in that state or bring us down even further.

Take a few minutes to think about this. It may be a point of view that nobody has offered you before. Perhaps you feel less valuable than other people not because you actually *are* less valuable, but because you have less power and strength to draw from than the people around you. Maybe you can't speak out about how you feel or protect yourself or function in an adult-like way because the energy that it would take for you to do that is just not there for you.

It's not that I want you to feel that you're off the hook here – you're not. If your source of power and strength is low, you still have to work to heal yourself and get well. I do, however, want you to know that it doesn't have to stay this way, that there is hope. And once you have the energy to feel more powerful, you can work on changing your behavioural patterns and adjusting the balance of power in your relationships.

The Energetics of Power vs Force

There is a significant difference between force and power and it's important not to confuse the two. There are many people in relationships who want to have everything the way they want it all the time. People like this use force to keep the other person in a position of submission. Over time, this results in the dominant person draining the power from the submissive person and it becomes harder and harder for the submissive person to break out of the relationship. You may recognize this pattern.

'I'm not able to finish my project at work. I can't focus. I know it should have been handed in weeks ago, but I always seem to find something more important to do. I'm so angry at myself about this. Maybe I'm not able to hold down a job, maybe I'm stupid – I don't know. My manager isn't happy with me, he keeps coming over to see why my project isn't finished yet and I can't answer him. This is very frustrating. I'm afraid I'll be fired.'

Marta has been coming to see me for a while, mostly because she is experiencing trouble at work. I ask her about her relationships with her family to track where the problem may have started.

'My father would yell at me a lot. I was never good enough for him. He always criticized me and I could never stand up to him. He made me feel that I couldn't do anything right.'

'This sounds a lot like the relationship between you and your manager,' I say. 'Do you think that your reaction to people in authority is based on your relationship to your father?'

Marta practically jumps out of her chair. 'Oh! I never thought of it like that – wow! I think you're right.' Her face lights up and her eyes brighten with hope. 'I'm always feeling that I'm not good enough for my manager – it's exactly the same thing!'

If you've been the submissive person in a power-based relationship, it can be difficult to speak your mind, to voice your opinion, your hurt or your discomfort with how you are being treated. Over time you may feel your voice is smaller and smaller, until you just give up completely and accept things as they are. You may feel you'll never have what you want, so you stop dreaming, stop creating the life you want and just go along with things to keep the peace. The problem with doing this is that you can build up resentment towards the people around you, have little tolerance or a snappy temper or, worse yet, disconnect from life altogether, as you feel there is no place for you in it, and fall into depression.

Know that it doesn't have to be this way. It can take some time for you to take your power back, but with determination, and the help I'm offering here, you could make changes that you would never have thought possible. Set your intention to be your most powerful self and know that it's okay to do that, and you'll soon be able to access your power and strength.

Your centre of power and strength is actually in your stomach, just below your belly button. It makes sense when you realize that's where you feel butterflies and nervous anxiety if you are worried. You may even find yourself so nervous at times you vomit up your food; people who are constantly suffering nervous anxiety often have stomach issues such as ulcers, acid reflux, IBS, diarrhoea or constipation. I find that when people relax in meditation, the gut relaxing only happens when they feel truly safe and comfortable. When your power and strength are fully restored to you, your stomach settles down and you can truly get in touch with your 'gut instinct' and use it as a tool for life.

Setting Your Intention

If you have a problem with the concept of power in that you have a limiting belief that power is bad, or dangerous, you have to start by transforming that. Force can be bad, aggression is bad; power is good, assertiveness creates healthy boundaries. Power is what drives you. Think of machinery or equipment, they need power to work, so do you. It's what you choose to do with your power that can be either healthy or unhealthy.

Once you're aware of your choices in any given situation and can respond, you can put your power to good use. But if you're caught up in a situation and don't take the time to become aware, you will react, and usually when we react it causes damage.

So, set your intention for the work in this chapter by saying the following affirmations out loud – *and mean them 100 per cent*:

* 'I no longer wish to live like this.'

* 'I give myself permission to take my power back.'

* 'I slow down and become more aware of my choices.'

* 'I choose to respond rather than react.'

* 'Power is my fuel. I deserve to have my power back.'

* 'Nobody can take my power away from me anymore.'

Say each one slowly, feeling its energy. Don't rush through them, stay with each one until you believe it, until you feel it in your bones 100 per cent. Allow your body to relax and check in with yourself as you repeat each one – how does it feel? Are you anxious? Is there a part of you that is afraid to change? Be with it, just as you did in the grounding exercise. Breathe with your anxiety, talk to it as if it were a child-like aspect of yourself, reassure it, tell it that everything is okay and it's time now to take your power back. Allow your anxiety to dissipate as you breathe out anything in your body that is reluctant or resistant to change.

Remember, being powerful doesn't mean that you will become a mean, nasty person. Gandhi was a very powerful man and the world also regards him as a very loving, tolerant man. When you are powerful you stand strong in your physical presence and aren't afraid to be fully in your body. You become someone other people look up to. You feel confident to make decisions, to try new things and to encourage others to do the same. You also allow yourself to make mistakes and give yourself the space to grow from those mistakes without beating yourself up about it. Being powerful means you don't let anyone treat you badly (including yourself) and you treat others the way you wish to be treated (this part takes practice). Being powerful means speaking your truth, even if you're aware that it may not be well received. Being true to yourself, true to your heart – there is power and freedom in that.

You Can Drain Your Own Power

As discussed above, other people can take your power from you. You can drain power from yourself too. I'm hoping that by this point in the book you've improved your relationship with yourself – however, we can always do a little more work on this!

The story we tell ourselves about something can drain our power, and the story usually isn't based on the truth but on an emotional charge we are carrying. For example, if you tell yourself you hate your job, just going into work can drain power from your energy body. But if you stop telling yourself you hate work and start focusing on something else instead, something you *don't* hate for example, then there is an energy shift. The amount of energy it takes to go into work, do the job and leave is very different from the amount of energy it takes to hate your job, go into work, hate being there and leave. By not actively hating your job you might have more energy to go look for a different job instead of being completely drained at the end of the day.

Ask yourself what stories you are telling yourself that are draining your power. Are you creating a story around an ex-partner that drains you just by thinking about them? Or do you feel a heaviness around a family member based on a story you keep telling yourself about them? People are people, they do what they do, however they do it. What makes them more powerful than you is when you give them your power by making assumptions that may not be the truth and are hurtful to you. If you've given them your power by creating a story around them that drains you, you can get it back quickly by destroying the story. In the next exercise I will show you how to do this.

I need to say from the outset that if the person you choose for this exercise is in an abusive relationship with you, it might not be appropriate for you to try the exercise with them. You might need to do more work on taking your power back first, so either skip this exercise and come back to it later or choose someone else to work with just for practice.

EXERCISE

Releasing People from the Story You Tell about Them

❖ Check in with your wellness scale first and notice if you're feeling any anxiety about this. If you feel a little fear, it's okay to do this exercise, but please don't do it if you have a high level of anxiety and a low feeling of wellness. Looking after yourself means not pushing yourself to do work you're not ready for.

❖ If you're ready, choose someone to work with in your mind's eye. Visualize them as you see them now. Let the colours, the energy around them reflect how you're feeling, so if you think this person is always angry, for example, see the anger dance around them like flames, or if you think they are grumpy or cranky, they could appear grey in colour and all tight in themselves, or with a cloud over their head. Let your soul show you how you are holding them in your energy field.

❖ Say out loud:

> *'I give myself permission to release my assumptions around [name in here], and by doing this, I clear the energy between us.'*

❖ Breathe and relax. Do you have 100 per cent permission? Can you give them the benefit of the doubt? If not, what is the issue? Is there something that is unfinished between you and this person? Make the decision to deal with it when you have more power available to you.

❖ Stay with it now, breathe again and imagine that as you breathe out, you are releasing the story you tell yourself about who they are and how they behave in the world and how they behave towards you. As you breathe in, relax more and more and trust that you are safe and well. Notice if your wellness scale naturally shifts upwards as you do this.

❖ As you breathe out, let assumptions about that person dissolve. Perhaps you can visualize the heavy energies around them falling away, the colours in the image softening and warming up and their face becoming calmer, more peaceful.

❖ Now, as you breathe in, breathe in energy of love, generosity and peace.

❖ As you continue to breathe, see the person relax and soften even more. See the energy charge around them so now they are just a person you know, without as much of an emotional 'charge' around them. Someone with their own issues, on their own journey. You might even feel that you can breathe love into the space between you.

❖ Then let the images dissolve away. Let them go completely and bring your awareness back to your body, back to the room. Know that the work has been done and something important has been cleared. Take as long as you feel you need to before going back to your day.

How do you feel after doing this? Relieved? Most of my clients love the feeling after this exercise, but it's important to realize that you've been creating the story around this person for much longer than you've been clearing the energy it has generated. Repetitive thoughts and old stories have a way of sticking with us if we don't pay attention to them, so even after doing this exercise you might find after a day or two you've recreated some of the heavy energy again. So do the exercise as many times as you need to until your thought patterns have also shifted. It will become easier as you go. Soon all you will have to do is think of the person and breathe out the energy you feel around them. Finally it will become light and easy, because you've really let it go.

You can adapt this exercise to situations too. If you think about work instead of a person, you might like to imagine the office you're in, or your manager, or even the pile of files on your desk. Or if you're anxious about a birthday party, a wedding or some family event, imagine how you feel about that and then clear your energies around it the same way. It's just a thing in space and time, and you're the one creating the stress, so you can let the stress go.

Powerful, eh?

✳✳✳✳

Reclaiming Your Power

I know you've all been waiting to get to this part! But it's really important for you to have done all the exercises and be familiar with the wellness scale before you launch into this particular exercise. The more grounded you are when you do this, the more effective it is. Please don't come to this exercise angry or emotional. Be in a calm state. It is what it is. It's nobody's fault. Remember, you're not a victim. Something in you allowed this to happen to you, and you're ready now to change that.

General Power Retrieval

This first exercise is a general power retrieval. You don't need to know where your power is returning from, you just want to take it back so you feel stronger and more powerful before doing further work.

EXERCISE

Reclaiming Your Power and Strength

This exercise has to be based on feeling from your essential self and not thinking from your mind. During it, whatever images, messages or thoughts come through you, notice if they are from your body (you'll feel them) or from your mind (usually these are a bit quicker to come in and are disconnected from your body). Go with what your body tells you.

❖ Take a wellness reading so you can compare before and after (and remember you can check in with your wellness scale as often as you wish).

❖ Create a safe, loving space for yourself where you can focus on this work. Turn off your phone. Light a candle or play some gentle music if you want, but it is not necessary.

❖ Sit upright with an open body posture and your feet on the ground. Breathe out your tiredness, your stress, anything that is distracting you from truly being present to this work.

❖ As you relax, bring your awareness into your body and drop down and down and down again, deep into your body, just as we did before.

- Notice when you feel centred and then continue and ground yourself below your feet into the Earth. Drop your energy cords deeply into the Earth, feel the connection and breathe the Earth energy back up into your body. Take as long as you need to do this.

- Now it's time to start reclaiming your power and strength. Press your feet into the ground and focus on your breath.

- As you breathe, focus on your stomach. Place your two hands there. How does it feel? Tight? Anxious? Breathe out any tightness, allow your stomach knots to unfold and loosen… See, feel and know that you are supported by the universe and you are safe.

- Now close your eyes and imagine a safe space in nature. This can be a beach, a forest, a meadow. What is the weather doing? How does the sky look? You're there, standing there holding a basket in your arms. Look around you, see where you are, what's there. Notice your basket – the materials, the texture. Notice what is beneath your feet. Now look up and say:

'I ask the universe to return my power
and strength to me. I'm ready.'

- Little balls of light start to appear in the landscape. These are parts of your power, the power that you have lost either by giving it away or by having someone take it from you. They will look different every time you do the exercise, depending on how you feel or what they are in relation to. They may appear as ribbons, or as leaves falling from the sky. They could appear as birds flying into a flock formation over your head before turning into a big ball of light. Just allow your power to appear in whatever form it chooses.

✦ You can gather the balls and place them in the basket you are holding. As you place them into your basket, they gel together; you can sense a warm glow coming from them. Catch them as they float through the breeze, climb up and retrieve the ones that are stuck in the leaves of the trees, find them under bushes or dancing in tall grasses. And if you can't reach one, ask it to come down gently into your basket. It will. No negotiation is required here.

✦ If it feels as though there are too many power balls for you to collect by yourself and you are becoming overwhelmed, that's okay. Just sit down in your landscape and breathe and be with it all. Come into balance with how much power you have lost. Then you can ask for help! Power animals or helpful healing energies will come to collect the balls for you. These energies may come in the form of rabbits, squirrels, birds, wolves... I've had clients who've had fairies, unicorns and dragons come! Wait and see what/who comes for you. It might even be another aspect of yourself, such as your inner child. Don't question it, just let it be; go with the flow of your imagination. Remember, it is your soul speaking to you, so sit back and enjoy it and know that it's for your highest good. These helpful energies can do all the work if you like, collecting the balls of light and dropping them into your basket of power and strength. Feel yourself getting heavier in your body as the basket gets filled. Feel loved, cherished and important. You are.

✦ Now, holding the basket close to your stomach, you're going to absorb all the power back into yourself. See the basket melt away so that now there is just one large ball of light floating in your lap. Allow it to dissolve into your stomach, into your energy field, dissolving into you, becoming part of you. Stay there with it and allow yourself to feel stronger, more powerful.

❖ Now you can let the all the images dissolve away too. Bring your awareness back into the room you are in. Feel your feet beneath you, become aware of your arms, your hands, your face, and when you are ready, you can go back to your day.

Taking back your power and strength brings a feeling of wholeness to your energy field. Check in with your wellness scale and see how you feel now.

Take some time to allow these energies to integrate, to bind together. It might even take a day or two. There is still more to do, but don't be in a rush. Giving yourself time to integrate these returning energies ensures that this work will be longer-lasting.

Reclaiming Your Power and Strength from a Relationship

After doing the previous exercise you may feel stronger than before, and that's wonderful. But, just like the previous exercises, the energy may 'leak out' again over time, so you may need to repeat it several times before you fully embody what you have lost. Let's go a bit deeper with this idea of power retrieval.

People you interact with over time, such as boyfriends/ girlfriends, parents or people at work, usually take some of your power and strength. Remember they don't do this on purpose and you have probably taken some from them, too. Subconsciously we are all playing our role and so the work to rewrite that role must also occur at the level of the subconscious, which is what we are doing here. Please don't judge during this exercise, or manufacture stories around the 'why/how', as that brings it all back to the mind and disrupts the flow of the work. Just go with it and feel the difference it is making to you, rather than thinking about who to blame.

EXERCISE

Reclaiming Your Power and Strength from Someone Else

You can do this exercise with someone in mind or you can do a general power retrieval from all your relationships, depending on how you are feeling. If you're working with a specific person in mind, make sure you feel safe to do so.

❖ Create a safe space to work as before. Relax, ground yourself, breathe. Allow your space in nature to appear in your mind's eye. Be at peace and know that everything will be okay. Connect into your stomach and make sure you're feeling safe.

❖ When you're ready, imagine the person you are reclaiming your power and strength from appearing in your landscape. If you feel vulnerable having them right there beside you, you could imagine they're on a movie screen instead. In any event, they can't talk to you unless you want them to. Remember you are working with their energy, not with their ego (personality) or their physical body.

❖ Some of your energy will be in their energy field. So, say:

> *'I call upon my power and strength to*
> *come back to me right now.'*

❖ Wait. See energy balls of light forming in that person's energy field, then lifting up and out of them and into the sky near you. Feel see and know that the power that is yours is being released and coming back to you as you asked.

❖ Let the balls of light, whatever their colour, gather together into a bigger ball. Now before you embody your power energy, you must cleanse it. Imagine rain falling onto the ball of light, for example, or that it goes for a dip in a lake or a river. You can ask for help to clean it from your power animals/energy helpers. A dragon power animal could breathe fire onto it, or birds could pick it clean.

❖ When the ball of light feels cleansed, allow it to come to you and receive it into your energy field, either absorbing it through the top of your head or allowing it to melt into your stomach as before, or just letting it go wherever it feels it needs to go. Stay with this part of the work as long as you are able.

❖ Just as with the energy retrieval we did earlier in the book, it's possible you're holding on to some of that person's power too. So think of this as an exchange, as a peace offering. Breathe and allow the balls of light that belong to them, if any, to rise up from you. See them being cleansed then going back to that person in a gentle way, and see the person relaxing and softening as they feel more like themselves again.

❖ You can close this exercise by having a conversation with the person. Think of it as your higher self talking to their higher self. Their ego won't hear you, but some aspect of them will, and they may even feel energy shift in themselves as a result and tension ease. So speak to them if you want to, say you are sorry things turned out this way and tell them you care about them but you can't continue to be in an unhealthy relationship. You may even hear them reply to you. Feel into it – not from your brain, remember! Whatever they say to you, it's okay. If they are upset and angry with you, perhaps it's you creating a story. The person's higher self will never be angry with you – it's only the personality that gets angry. So step back and let it unfold naturally, rather than make it up or try to force something. Give thanks for the conversation, Then, when you're ready, allow their image to dissolve away from your landscape.

- Take a minute or two to come into balance. You might want to visualize yourself jumping into a lake or a river in your landscape to wash away any debris or any emotion that came up for you as your energy returned. You don't need it and you don't want to bring it back with you. You can also ask your power animals/energy helpers to help you recalibrate and come into balance.

- When you're ready, let the landscape dissolve away and bring your awareness fully back into the room you're in. Take a break and let the energies settle.

You can repeat this exercise if you wish, either with the same person or with someone else.

All of this connecting to other people's energy fields is done subconsciously; our brain is not aware of it. We're bringing our awareness in when we do work like this, but not everyone knows how to do it. So, if you do this exercise then telephone your mother and tell her she was holding on to your power and strength and you've taken it all back from her, she won't know what you're talking about, and she might get upset about it. It's not a conversation you can really have with someone. Know, though, that the other person may well feel different after you do this. They may even feel better and stronger, as now they can connect to their own power and strength instead of pulling on and depending on yours. And this opens up the possibility of a change in the dynamics in the relationship between you both, for the better.

> *When we complete the exercise for Marta and her father, Marta is peaceful for several minutes. Then she opens her eyes and her face is bright, her smile is wide.*
>
> *'I've never felt like this before,' she says. 'I want to get up and stretch.'*
>
> *'So do it!' I say.*
>
> *She gets up from the chair and stretches her arms up to the sky.*
>
> *'I feel about six feet tall now,' she says. 'And heavy! Solid in my body. Wow. I feel stronger. Wonderful!'*
>
> *That night, she told me later, her father phoned her unexpectedly and asked how she was. He listened to her and didn't criticize. He'd never done that before.*

Don't have expectations that a relationship will change overnight when you do this work. But keep doing it and over time *you* will shift, even if the other person doesn't.

You will become more aware of your boundaries and your subconscious will respect them, making it much less likely that you will be drained by anyone.

Clearing Unwanted Behaviour in Relationships

When you've been the submissive person in a relationship for years and then suddenly you get your power back, you'll start to see things in the relationship that you really can't tolerate any longer. It can be as if someone has taken off a blindfold you've been wearing and you can see what has been going on for the first time. You might be surprised or shocked, and you might find yourself reverting to your old behaviour and old patterns because you don't know what else to do. This is normal and natural, so please don't be worried or anxious about it. Know that you will have time to work on it, but you also need to know that you will make mistakes. Don't be angry at yourself when this happens, see it all as learning.

So the unwanted behaviour I'm talking about here doesn't belong to the other party, but to you. Take a moment for this to sink in. Because now you have to be responsible in the relationship. You're no longer the victim, remember?

The rest of this chapter is dedicated to helping you become aware of what might happen when you become more powerful in your relationships, and I'll give you some tools and techniques to help you feel more in control of how you respond to situations. Please look after yourself, and again, you might need to seek professional help if this chapter has brought up a lot of issues that you didn't realize were impacting on your life. Don't forget about the resources at the back of the book to help you find a good therapist.

Sometimes you need to talk things out with someone else to really make sense of them and get centred and balanced in your life.

What is Unwanted Behaviour?

So let's be clear what I'm talking about. There are many different forms of unwanted behaviour, but it usually comes in the form of self-sabotage. You can either set yourself up to get hurt so that you can blame the other person for hurting you, or you can blame yourself for messing something up. It can be so subtle you don't even realize you're sabotaging yourself until afterwards, when you blame yourself for 'doing it again', whatever 'it' may be. Aha! That's it.

Unwanted behaviour can also occur in the form of submission, where you allow a person to exert control over you in a relationship. This is not something I can deal with here to the degree that you might need to solve things completely for you, so take as much as you can from what I'm saying and, I can't say it enough, get help if you feel overwhelmed.

The key is to value yourself more, to realize that you don't have to put yourself down, that you deserve happiness in life; to stop being a victim and become responsible for your self-care and for your own behaviour in relationships. This would be a good time to go back to the self-worth exercise in the previous chapter (*see page 99*) and do it again. After all the power-retrieval work you've just done, it's good to check in with yourself, get your bearings, maybe write in your journal. Getting well is hard work, but I have every faith that you can do it.

Disempowering Thoughts Are a Form of Self-Sabotage

Feeling confident that you are good at something is a reflection of your self-worth. One of my clients, Samantha, was an art student, and she had an internal battle between wanting to get recognition and not allowing herself to receive it. When her disempowering thoughts kicked in, her unwanted behaviour pattern was to 'rub her own nose in it' to prove that she didn't deserve success. Sounds complicated perhaps, but it's a very common type of self-sabotage. After working with me in session, Samantha was able to notice her thoughts and see the pattern, but she still felt trapped in it. It was as if she split off from herself – part of her was having the thoughts and then acting out of those thoughts, while the other part was observing it all.

> 'I handed in my assignment and actually apologized to my tutor! I told him I'd done a really bad job. I heard myself saying the words and I couldn't believe it! I was so embarrassed, but I just kept on talking, making excuses for how bad my work was. I felt myself shrink inside. When he looked at it and told me that it wasn't as bad as I'd made it out to be, I had trouble hearing that. I couldn't feel better about it – it was as though some part of myself just wouldn't let me hear something good about myself.'

There's lots going on here. First of all, as Samantha found, being aware of your disempowering thoughts and sabotage patterns doesn't enable you to break out of them right away. Expect that you will have a learning curve to get through on this process. It is so important not to judge yourself during it. The worst thing you can do is go into more disempowering thoughts such as *I'm such an idiot, why do I behave like this? I wish I didn't do this.* Doing that keeps you stuck in your pattern.

What should you do? When you feel yourself shrink inside, notice it. You can use energy healing to come back to your normal size. Embarrassment causes your energy to contract. So if this does happen to you, find some space and breathe, use the exercises for centring and grounding (*see pages 82 and 87*), come back into your body and tell yourself that you'll be okay. Breathe out the embarrassment and reassure yourself that you're still learning. You can even say 'Well done!' to yourself for noticing it. I have some power statements later on in this chapter that you can use for reassurance (*see page 132*).

Relationships that trigger self-sabotage patterns are most likely to be intimate relationships such as mother–daughter, boyfriend–girlfriend, or relationships with someone in authority, such as a manager, a teacher or even a policeman. If you have had low self-worth for a long time, being submissive in the relationship was possibly a method of survival for the child-like aspect of yourself, but now it's time to grow into your full potential as an adult. You can do it!

Start by Forgiving Yourself

You didn't get this way intentionally. Learning how you are wired doesn't mean you have another excuse to blame yourself for something! When you realize that you've acted out, you need to take some time out to come back into balance with yourself. Forgive yourself as best you can, with understanding and compassion. The child-like aspect of you felt safer doing whatever it was that you did, but you don't need to behave like this any longer.

Here are some affirmations to help you. You can say them out loud. Make sure you mean them 100 per cent. It can be hard to mean them if you're not used to it. But you'll get there.

* 'I forgive myself for sabotaging myself.'

* 'I no longer wish to cause myself emotional pain.'

* 'Every day I learn to love myself a little bit more.'

* 'I am patient and tolerant with myself.'

* 'I am committed to my healing process.'

See how none of these create a huge gap for you to fall into? Yet they can be affirmations you can say for the rest of your life, if you need to. They grow with you. So stick with one or two of them and say them as many times as you need to until you eliminate any doubt around whether or not you believe them.

If you're having trouble with this, go back to the self-worth exercise and do that again, then come back here and try this one again. Your persistence will pay off in the end.

Changing the Energy You Are Holding around a Situation

The emotion you feel after a situation in which you expressed unwanted behaviour may be embarrassment, shame, guilt or anger. These are the heaviest and slowest energies of all, and, boy, do they weigh you down. Because you're more aware of this now, you might make it worse for yourself by placing additional pressure on yourself to handle things better. But remember, Samantha saw herself acting out, knew she was doing it and still was unable to change it. Give yourself time to work on this, as it doesn't happen quickly.

When situations haven't gone the way we wanted them to, our tendency is to replay them over and over again in our mind. What happens when we do this is we create more of the energy that we don't want in our life. The best thing to do is to focus on releasing the unwanted energies rather than creating more. You can turn it around by breathing out the heavy energies, doing the grounding exercises (*see pages 82 and 87*) and going for a walk, allowing the anxiety and stress to leave your body. Reaffirm that you are healing and in process, that you are still learning and that your life is getting better every day. When you feel more grounded, take it further with the next exercise.

EXERCISE

Changing How You Hold the Energy of Something That Happened

❖ Play back the incident in your mind, as if you're watching it on video. Just before you say whatever it was that you wish you hadn't said, press pause. While the image is in freeze-frame, you can zoom in, zoom out, make yourself bigger than the other person and make yourself smaller. You can use this to take the energy charge out of the situation. Make the image black and white, reverse the colours, do whatever you need to do with the skills you have now to neutralize the situation and remove the emotional charge.

❖ How do you feel about it now? Less embarrassed/upset/powerless? If not, do it again. Keep working on it until you don't feel any emotional charge around the situation. (Yes, this might even mean walking away from the exercise, then coming back to it a few hours or even a day or so later.)

❖ What would you like to have been the outcome of this situation? What do you think you would have said, if you had been able to? Press 'play' again on the memory and change it so that you say what you think you should have said. Allow the memory to shift, so that the person in the relationship with you changes their response to you. See things coming into balance, feel the energy shifting.

❖ How do you feel now? How would you feel if that person walked into the room where you are right now? Maybe you'd like to write down your thoughts. Know that you've processed this event, and if your mind brings it back to you again, even after doing this exercise, you can gently say to this aspect of yourself, 'Thank you. Yes, I did get upset about this, but I've processed it and I can move on.' Repeat this as many times as you need to, so you avoid 'polluting' the energy further.

✳✳✳✳

You won't always get your way in reality and the purpose of this exercise is not to brainwash you into thinking that everything is wonderful. What happened still happened the way it happened, but you can allow yourself to feel less upset about it. Think of this as training for the next time. You might want to do the power-retrieval exercise again too (*see page 116*). These are powerful exercises, and as you do them more frequently, you may even be able to catch yourself in a situation in the moment and realize you have the opportunity to change your pattern then and there.

Creating the New Empowered You

Before you let go of unwanted behaviour, it helps to recognize what type of behaviour you do want. Take some time to write about this in a journal. You could do it logically, by writing out what you have done in the past and then beside it what you would like to do now. Be specific, go back to different situations that stick out for you and then, instead of remembering what happened, visualize the healed you behaving in a new way.

Be clear in your head about what it is you want to create. This isn't about getting revenge or being able to give as good as you get. You are learning how to be empowered, to keep your boundaries clear, and to give and receive the respect in relationships that we all deserve. Power statements may help you here.

Using Power Statements

Power statements are statements that are said out loud to another person when you need to deliver a message loud and clear. They help you set strong boundaries.

Here is a list of power statements that I have used myself and with clients. You may need to learn them word for word at first, until you are more confident and feel that they come naturally to you. They're about setting boundaries, remember, and when your boundaries are stronger, you will be stronger in your power.

Pick one or two that resonate with you to start with – don't use them all at once. You might immediately want to rewrite them for your own situation. Great! Go do it. Ease yourself into it like a very hot bath. Practise saying the power statements out loud. Imagine yourself saying them in a particular situation. Can you feel the energy changing?

* 'When you scream at me, it makes me feel anxious and then I'm not able to properly answer your question.'

* 'I'm not able to give you an answer right now. I will think about it and get back to you.'

* 'I will review what you have said and respond to it when I am able to.'

* 'I would prefer to speak to you about this when you are not angry.'

* 'I am only prepared to take 50 per cent of the blame here, as there are two of us involved.'

If you get through to the person and they hear what you have to say, it's a success. If you slow down the conversation, it's a success. If you don't revert to your unwanted behaviour, it's a success. Even the smallest shift from your old pattern is a success.

Be big in your energy in your interactions. Do your power-retrieval exercises, do your cord-cutting exercises and stay grounded. Each time you have an interaction, something else will have shifted. Remember that you are just as valid and just as important as anyone else.

If you feel very uncomfortable with the power statements, you may need to get some professional help. You're worth it, so don't hesitate to call someone. Psychotherapists who work with cognitive behavioural therapy (CBT) and coaches who use neuro-linguistic programming (NLP) for conflict management/negotiation skills use statements much like these. A few sessions with someone like this could be a great complement to the work that you have been doing so far in this book.

Transforming Unwanted Behaviour

To transform unwanted behaviour as it is happening, you have to become aware of it, break the energy flow and then introduce new behaviour. Your learned way of reacting will have been based on your need for survival, so breaking the flow may take a lot of energy. It can feel like a leap into the unknown, but it's so worth it.

> *Andy's mother is a constant source of upset. She tells everyone how terrible it is that Andy hasn't moved out of the house yet, that he isn't up for that promotion, that his girlfriend has left him for someone else. And even when he's in the room, she will talk about him to others as if he isn't there. Andy is 35. He just can't take it anymore.*

> *'I just clam up, I can't speak ... I feel it like daggers in my heart. I know what she is saying is putting me down, but I can't stand up for myself.'*

We do some power-retrieval exercises, we cut cords and Andy's rating on the wellness scale improves. We plan out new behaviour and write power statements, but things don't seem to change in his relationship with his mother.

'What would happen if you stood up for yourself?' I ask him. 'What are you afraid of most?'

'I think it's hurting Mum's feelings. If I tell her she's in the wrong, that will upset her.'

'Isn't she upsetting you, too? Aren't you just as important and valid a person as she is?'

'Yes, you're right,' Andy sighs. 'I really have to do this for my own sanity.'

At our next session, he says, 'I talked to Mum in private and used my power statement: "When you talk about me as if I'm not in the room, it makes me feel that you don't care about me." She said she didn't know what I was talking about.'

He shakes his head, but smiles.

'Wait till I tell you what happened next. It was her birthday party last week. She was doing it again, telling her friends all about how I forgot to pick up the dry-cleaning so she couldn't wear her favourite dress to the party, then telling everyone how I got the wrong type of cream for the dessert. I felt myself shrinking back, my usual pattern, but then I remembered my power statement. I sat up straight in the chair and gritted my teeth, but the urge to speak out was stronger than ever, so I took the risk.'

'What did you say?' I ask.

'I just said, "Stop talking about me as if I am not here."
That's it. The whole room was silenced. She heard me say it.
She didn't apologize, but she couldn't deny it this time. I felt
elated! I didn't die from saying it! I will do it again. I might
even use one of the other power statements too!'

After putting in a lot of work, Andy has now been able to
change his unwanted behaviour in the relationship with
his mother. Instead of shrinking into the background, he
is speaking out. His success has resulted in an increase in
his self-worth, which has increased his self-esteem. Only six
months later, he has a new job and has moved out.

Responding Instead of Reacting

Every relationship is different, and unwanted behaviour in relationships is also different, depending on the dynamics of what's happening. But when we react by going back to old patterns, it is usually because we feel under pressure. We don't give ourselves the space we need to think about what's happening and what we want to achieve. And with low self-worth, it can feel that we don't deserve the space or aren't allowed to ask for it. But we do deserve it and we can ask for it.

Response Ability: the ability to respond.

Someone else's urgency, anger or emotional pain doesn't belong to us and we aren't responsible for it. We are only responsible for ourselves. When in an argument or a conflict with someone who wants to get their own way, the first thing we have to do is *slow everything down.*

This can be an issue if, for example, someone is asking us to do something and our body is telling us a big 'no' but we're not able to say 'no' to that person. Have you ever been in that position?

Don't say 'yes' straightaway just to keep everyone happy. Setting healthy boundaries means being able to say 'no' if 'no' is the correct answer for you.

Ask yourself what's going on. And ask the person to repeat what they said if you need to, so you can be clear about exactly what it is they want from you.

Now take the space you need. It can help to ground yourself while you do this. Breathe and visualize your energy field growing bigger (remember how Samantha felt small?) When you get big, you take up more space. You can slow down even more if you want to. You might need to use a power statement to get some space, or an affirmation in your mind to support yourself as you do this. Ask yourself if you're making up a story or if how you are feeling is the truth. If you feel under pressure, clear this pressure with your intention, then breathe out everything in you that feels like pressure, and feel your feet flat on the ground and your connection to the Earth.

You might know exactly what you want to say in response once you are centred and in balance, so wait until you are and then say it clearly and calmly, rather than in a way that is charged with emotion. If you don't know what you want to say in response, know that you don't have to answer right away. Unless there is a real emergency, it's only their urgency that is pushing you for an answer right now. You *don't* have to give an answer right away, even if the other person makes you feel that you do. You have the right to say something like 'I'll think about it and get back to you when I have an answer.' They really can't argue with that. Try using some of your power statements if it feels appropriate.

Stay slow, stay big and the dynamics will change. When you're slow, you have more control over your behaviour. You may still make mistakes. Forgive yourself and keep doing your work. You're still learning and you're doing great.

Chapter 5

Healing Your Inner Wounds

'No matter where we live on the planet or how difficult our situation seems to be, we have the ability to overcome and transcend our circumstances.'
LOUISE HAY

'If you try to get rid of fear and anger without knowing their meaning, they will grow stronger and return.'
DEEPAK CHOPRA

Everything we have done together in this book so far has been to help you clear and heal your current life situation so that you can be more connected to yourself and enjoy a better quality of life. What we are going to do now is look inwards and start to clear out some of the old wounding and trauma you may still hold in both your physical body and your energy body, so that you can feel lighter and happier at a deeper level.

The work in this chapter needs you to take a different approach: here we go deep. Now I'm not going to assume that you've mastered all we've done up to this point. It takes years to master this type of work and we are all works in progress. So you might feel happier stopping for a while until you feel the baseline level on your wellness scale has stabilized at a higher value. Just make sure your discomfort isn't about resistance to doing your work; we all have to push ourselves a little bit to go deeper from time to time.

As the work we are about to do will visit deep inner wounding, please, if you've not done work on this before, go gently. Visit your wellness scale frequently, and *if you're below 5, don't do any of the exercises in this chapter.* Work on getting yourself back up to at least a 7 or an 8 and then come back and do one of the exercises and see how you go. You may need support if old emotions come up, and you might become fragile and vulnerable as you clear some of the 'junk' out of your 'river'. So be aware, and put your health ahead of your zeal to clear all your junk quickly. There's plenty of time – you have the rest of your life.

Your Energy Field Is Like a River

A flowing river is a great metaphor for your personal energy field. You can imagine that all the things that have caused you emotional pain are clogging the flow of energy in your field, just like rubbish clogging a river.

Most rivers have rubbish in them, such as plastic bottles, glass or paper. Some contain bits of broken trees and the occasional dead animal. I have seen rivers with shopping trolleys, broken bits of concrete, even cars thrown in after accidents or storms. The contents of a river depend upon what has happened during its lifetime and where it is situated. Some rivers are completely clogged with rubbish and hardly flow at all.

Even a flowing river isn't free of obstacles. All rivers have rocks and stones on the riverbed. Obstacles are part of life.

When you start to pull rubbish out of a river, the rubbish around it becomes dislodged, the water around it becomes cloudy and heavy, and there is some disruption before the river settles and runs clear. This is similar to the healing process. It takes time, and once you start, other things come up that you might not have expected. But it's all in the cause of creating a cleaner, healthier, faster-flowing river, so if that's what you're looking for, it's got to be done.

Starting Your Internal Work

Even if you think you've already dealt with trauma, it might only have been at one level, most likely the mental layer. Your energy could still be holding onto it even though you have worked through all the logic around what happened. So don't be surprised if you find you're still carrying emotional pain around something you've worked on already.

In this chapter I will outline some tools and techniques to help you clear some of your internal wounding, blockages and stuck energy. Read through them and pick one to try, but don't try more than one on the same day. You can repeat each technique as many times as you like. Know that it will be different each time. And it's so important to take your time with this – you need to allow those waters to settle before you dig some more!

You may also need to get help if you feel stuck. That's okay, we all need help from time to time. We're not always able to hoist a car out from a river by ourselves. There are many ways to extract a car from a river – you can go in there and take a hammer and a chainsaw to it, hack it up into smaller pieces and pick those out bit by bit, or you could also ask someone with a small crane to come by and help you lift the whole thing out in one go. I'm not recommending either of these methods, because only you know what is best for you. You might not be ready to see the whole car as it is hoisted out and smaller bits over time might be easier for you to manage. However, if you're tired of this big old car being there, getting rid of it in one go could be the way for you. Don't worry, you don't need to make any decisions now. Once you are familiar with the exercises, you will be able to decide what you need when the time comes.

Before you start, it's helpful to know how much work you have to do, so let's take a look at your river now.

Damage Assessment

If you are a river flowing from your birth up to this present moment, how much 'rubbish' is blocking your flow? Take a few minutes right now to do an assessment.

EXERCISE

River Visualization

You'll need to drop down into your body to do this exercise, so switch off outside distractions for a while and create a quiet space. Breathe, come into your body and relax. Imagine your spiritual essence is gathering around your physical body as you get ready to do this work. See it forming a ball of light above your head and wait until you feel present and ready to start.

✦ With each breath, visualize the ball of light dropping down a little bit more into your body, starting at your head (breathe) and dropping into your mouth (breathe), your neck (breathe), your chest (breathe) and your heart (rest here for at least three breaths).

✦ Ask your soul to show you a river that represents you and the amount of emotional pain you are carrying in your energy field. When you see the river, remember it's okay, it is as it is supposed to be and you are able to handle it. It might come as a shock. That's also okay, just be with it. Sit with the image of the river and allow yourself to come into balance and accept the amount of work you have to do. Know that this may be just one layer of it, the layer that you are going to work with now, and as you clear this layer, there may be another one beneath.

✦ If you feel able to, look more closely at the clutter and the rubbish. Do you know what all the bits and pieces represent? Here are some possibilities:

- A crashed car could be a huge trauma in your life that you've not really got over.

- Broken trees could be limiting beliefs that someone put in there. (Limiting beliefs are beliefs that limit your capability, such as 'I'm not good enough' or 'I'll never be able to do that.)

- Large rocks and stones wedged in the riverbed could represent limiting beliefs that you've created based on your life experiences.

✦ Know, though, that you are unique and only you know what your 'rubbish' is. If you want to ask your body what a particular item is about, go ahead. The body knows.

- How is the health of the land around the river? What is the weather like? What else do you see? All of this could be connected to your wellness scale.

- When you're ready, gently bring your awareness back into the room.

It would be very useful for you to take your notebook at this point and write down how you feel, what you learned and whether you feel better or worse now that you are more aware of the state of your energy.

Once you have done some work on your river, you can come back and reassess it. Know that it will change as you commit to being well.

✳✳✳✳

It can come as quite a shock to see the rubbish that you've been carrying around with you. Do remember that you've been functioning in your life up to this point with all that stuff in there and your life will get even better as you start to clear it.

What to Expect

This work will probably not be as easy and quick as some of the other work you've done. A lot depends on where you are on your journey. What it really takes is commitment to do the work. If you have the intention to heal, you will find healing everywhere – in a book, in a conversation with a friend or in simply a quiet moment when you're ready to let go of something. If you're resisting healing, then you have to work with the resistance first.

Healing deep wounds isn't straightforward. If you were to remove a deeply embedded shopping trolley or car wreck from a river, there would be a bit of upset and turmoil until the water settled and cleared again. This may happen to you, too. Some of my clients get a bit dizzy when they get a strong burst of energy flowing as they release something that has been there for a long time. Sometimes they get upset or even angry.

Sarah says, 'My life doesn't have purpose or meaning anymore. I'm angry all the time and I don't know why. I threw away a lot of my books because they didn't help me. I don't know who to trust anymore, there's so much information out there. I'm so confused ... I can't sleep, I'm eating too much, I'm not interested in anything. It's as though I'm homesick for somewhere I've never been. Maybe I don't belong here. I'm worried I might be depressed.'

We do a deep clearing, removing some very old emotional blocks.

When she comes back to see me two weeks later, she is anxious and agitated.

'I don't think I'm any better. I feel trapped like an animal in a cage ... I was great after our session, but two days later the anger came back and it was even worse than before. I don't know what to do. I'm so disappointed that this healing didn't work.'

'How do you know it didn't work?' Maybe you're supposed to be angry now? Does the anger feel the same as the anger you had before?'

'Actually no, this anger is angrier, if that makes any sense...'

'What would it be like for you if you just let yourself be angry instead of fighting it?'

She sighs. Starting to settle, she says, 'Well, I am angry. Furious, in fact. How could I have been treated that badly?' After some talking (and more healing), she eventually says, 'I know I did the best that I could. I wish I could have done more, but I didn't.'

I say, 'You weren't the same person back then – you weren't able to do any more than you did. It's safe now to forgive yourself and move on.'

This case study is the equivalent of hoisting a big bit of debris out of the river and deciding whether you want to keep it or throw it away. You can get angry by just looking at it, angry at whoever has put it there, even angry at yourself for allowing it to be thrown in. But holding it up and examining it, turning it around and around to look for more information isn't useful, in fact it just makes it bigger and heavier and harder to let go of.

Sarah is still struggling. 'But I've been so angry about this for so long now, I don't know what it would be like not to be angry anymore.'

It takes time to come into balance with healed energy. You may feel different, freer, as if there's a space that wasn't there before. But remember, this new space could be filled with anything at all, and if you're not focused on what you're going to fill it with, you could end up filling it with something similar to what was there before. Sometimes you need to make sense of what you're letting go of in order to make way for something new. You may also need to grieve before you're ready to truly let it go. It's all part of the process.

> *'You are here now, in this life, this body,' I say, 'with an opportunity to be happy right in front of you. Do you want to take it or do you want to continue to live in fear and anger?'*

> *Sarah sighs. 'I know you're right. Maybe I'm just scared of being happy. I don't know what that will be like. But it's exciting too.'*

> *'Why not let yourself be angry but also let yourself be happy if you feel happy? Maybe one day you won't be angry anymore.'*

Like Sarah, you might find yourself unable to let go of the pain because it's so familiar to you. This is beautiful but sometimes difficult work. So be patient with yourself. Give yourself plenty of time and space and extra support. If you don't feel that you're able to do it right now, know that it's here for you when you're ready.

Pick One Thing to Heal: Set Your Intention

With your river in mind, begin by changing one thing and one thing only. What do you choose to let go of? Picking one thing to transform is very do-able, it is not overwhelming and it leaves a feeling of achievement afterwards: you've taken another step closer to being well. And once you remove one thing, it is possible that it can dislodge or loosen others, just as in a river, so that one thing may lead to several other items being cleared from your energy at once.

Take some time before you start any of the exercises in the next part of this chapter and pick one thing that you'd like to clear from your energy field. Have a read through the techniques and use your intuition to pick the one that feels right to you, based on your intention.

Know that there are two ways of working. You can either recognize what it is you need to change in this physical world and take some action to clear it (i.e. needing to forgive someone or be forgiven), or you can visualize your river (from the damage assessment we did earlier) and choose to remove one item from that, without needing to know what it represents. Or do both. When you work energetically, you don't need to go back and re-experience the trauma to heal it. You'll know what you need to do.

Techniques for Clearing Your Energy Field of Deeper Wounding

This next section gives you some techniques to help you clear out your inner wounds. Just like the exercises we did earlier in the book, you will need to repeat these over time to get the maximum effect.

Cleaning Out the River

You can use this exercise anytime. It is a great way to release built-up emotion around thought patterns and memories. It also helps you to imprint a healed image into your energy field as you relax your body and let go.

EXERCISE

Clearing Out the River

✦ Close your eyes, drop down into your body, breathe slowly and take your time. Make sure you are grounded and centred. This part of this exercise could take you at least 5–10 minutes. If you want to do big healing work, stay with it for longer if you can before you get started. The more relaxed you are, the deeper the work will be.

✦ Drop down into your heart, breathe and stay there for a while. Do the energy-clearing exercise (see page 46). You can also do the tie-cutting exercise (see page 62) if you wish.

✦ Visualize your river as it is now. Imagine you're there, beside it, just observing it. Spend time by the water until you feel that you've really arrived there. Step into the water if you want to. Swim in it. Feel how cold it is, how quickly it moves. Allow your essential self, your soul, to show you everything in your energy field that can be cleared and healed. Wait until you feel that you have a true image.

✦ You can stay where you are and pick out some debris if that's what you feel called to do, or you can follow the course of the river towards the source, going back in time. You can see yourself moving rocks, stones and boulders out of the water. You can find aspects of yourself showing up to help you clear the river. If it feels overwhelming, you could invite other healing energies to help too; they may come in the form of power animals/angels/guides/ancestors, even fairies, mermaids and unicorns! Just go with it, see what/who comes. They are all good high-vibrational helpers.

❖ Spend as long clearing your river as you are able to. When you've had enough and are ready to come back, you might like to have a rest on the riverbank and just admire your work. Ask for your own energy to be cleansed so that you don't bring any of the debris back with you. This is very important: *don't* cleanse yourself in your own river; instead, walk away from it and find a different body of water such as a lake, or even the sea to jump in, or feel the sunshine burn away any debris or heavy energy you have picked up during the work. Fire could also burn away the debris. The wind can blow it away too.

❖ Feel renewed, lifted, lighter in your body as you look at the river, which is flowing more quickly, strongly and clearly. Take a moment to imagine that the water is getting even clearer, the colours brighter, that the river is glowing with health and vitality, and so are you. Feel light shining brightly in your physical body – your heart, your stomach, your legs, your arms.

❖ When you're ready, disconnect from the image of the river completely and let it dissolve away. Start to bring your awareness back into your body, into the room where you are. Come slowly back into your physical body. Feel your arms and legs, your hands and feet. Become aware of your breath.

❖ Don't jump up and rush about – take as long as you need to come into balance with your higher vibration. You might want to write down what you experienced, what you learned. Have a cuppa and a rest – you've earned them.

✳✳✳✳

Healing an Aspect of Yourself

Many aspects of you exist in this moment in time, even though you may feel there's only one you! We talked before about your mind, your emotions, your thoughts, your body and your essential self. But within your essential self there are also many parts – you when you were a baby, you when you were a child, a teenager, and so on. If a part of you didn't get what it needed when it needed it, it became what you might call frozen in time. You may have many of these unfulfilled parts and they may show up in your behaviour when you least expect it. You might find yourself acting out of child-like anger if you don't get your way in a relationship, for example.

In this next healing technique, you create a gentle, safe space and invite an aspect of yourself that needs healing to come forward. Each time you do this, the aspect that shows up may be different from before. It may appear as a younger version of you, it may appear as an animal or a mythological creature and it may not look like you at all. Why is this? It's the energy of the aspect expressing itself in the best way it knows. Don't judge it, just be gentle and loving, ask what it needs from you and how you can support it better, and give it as much love as you are able. I have this exercise available as a downloadable recording on my website if you want me to guide you through it.

Exercise

Healing an Aspect of Yourself

❖ In a safe and quiet space, with all distractions removed, set your intention. You can say out loud: 'I disconnect from my mind, from external things and from what I think I need. I ask to be guided by my inner wisdom to meet the aspect of myself that needs healing today.' As you get more used to doing this exercise over time, you may want to word your intention differently, and that's okay.

❖ Ground and centre yourself in your body. Breathe. Be as present in your body as you can. Feel your spiritual essence filling your body; feel as if each cell in your body is waking up and giving this process its full attention. If you're thinking about other things or anticipating who will show up, you're not in the right space and may have to try again later.

❖ When you are truly relaxed, visualize a safe space in nature. Notice what it's like, where you are, what is underfoot. What can you smell? Touch? Taste? What is the weather doing? Are you on a beach, in a forest, on a mountain? Wherever you are, relax and explore the space until you feel comfortable there.

❖ Find a clearing with some trees and a marble bench. Go there and sit down and wait. The aspect of you that needs healing today will come to visit you there when it feels right.

❖ When it arrives, say hello. Notice how it's feeling, its body language. Ask if it needs anything from you right now. What can you do to help? Then be quiet and listen. Let it talk to you, if it is able. It might just want to show you something or simply be in your awareness. It might take you by the hand and take you on a journey – go and learn. Open your heart to this aspect of yourself, get to know it better. As angry or as upset as you or it may be, there's healing to be done here. Be real, be gentle – your intention is to heal. So, forgive. Love. Cherish. Share. Hug. Don't fight or argue. That does damage. Stay with this aspect of yourself until you feel the space between you soften, until you feel love come in. You might not get a complete resolution of the issue, but any progress is good. You can come back and visit it again and make further progress.

❖ When you're ready to say goodbye, if it's appropriate, embrace the aspect of yourself that you've been working with. Give thanks to it for showing up and to the energies around you for facilitating the healing.

❖ To make sure you don't bring back any heavy emotional energies, cleanse yourself by jumping into a crystal lake/ the sea and let the water wash you clean. Alternatively, you can invite the wind or rain to wash you clean. You can stand under the bright warm sun and dry off.

❖ Make sure you feel comfortable and clear in yourself, rested and relaxed, then connect in with your heart, with your physical body, come back to the room you're in and let the images gently dissolve away.

❖ Stretch your arms and your legs, and when you're ready, open your eyes.

❖ You can again write everything down, if you wish. Take a rest before going back into your daily activities.

If you have promised the aspect of yourself that you will do something for it, such as have more fun in your life or leave a bunch of flowers on the grave of your grandmother, you will have to honour your promise.

Whenever you sit down to do this work, have no expectations of whom you may meet. Even the space in nature may change as your energy shifts to a higher vibration. But as long as you are coming from your heart, not your head, this exercise will help you clear your energy field.

As you get more comfortable and confident doing this work, you will find that you become lighter in yourself, have fewer mood swings and are able to set better boundaries. As more aspects of yourself feel heard, held and validated, you will feel more contained, more like the responsible, healed person you are becoming.

Forgive Everyone, Even Yourself

Sometimes we tend to hold a grudge about something that has long been over. We may still be upset with the person/ people involved or even ourselves for how we behaved at the time. It's important to clear all these grudges, as they taint your energy field with lower vibrations such as guilt, shame, resentment, jealousy and anger. Some are easier to let go of than others; some of them may have got way deep under your skin and be lying in your bones, just waiting quietly to show up in your life one day.

There are two different types of issue here: finished business and unfinished business.

❈ *Finished business* is where all that needs to be said has been said, resolution has been reached and you could walk away and know you did all you could do but you still feel the energy in your body. It may be finished business between you and the other party, but inside you it is not yet complete.

❈ *Unfinished business* is something that is still ongoing, where you feel that you need to say your piece or be heard by someone who isn't listening to you. There are actually two types of unfinished business:

～ issues that are active in your life right now

～ old issues that happened a long time ago and 'went away' but aren't really gone – perhaps they crop up from time to time or you find little things act as a trigger for them

Let's clear the energies around how you hold all of these issues now. This is a two-part exercise: the first part is brain work, the second is energy work.

Exercise

Forgive Everyone: Part I

✦ Catalogue all your past history – you may need a pen and paper for this. Travel back in time in your mind and allow all your past relationships to show up in your awareness. How do you feel about these relationships? Give yourself permission to feel it in your body. Old boyfriends/

girlfriends, teachers, parents, even friendships that went wrong somehow... Write a list of the people that you feel you still hold resentment around, a list of people you need to forgive. This can include people who have passed away too. It's about what *you* are holding in your energy field, not about them. No matter whether they are living or dead, if you hold uncomfortable energy, possibly in the form of a grudge, around them, write it down.

❖ Now it's about you. Track back in time to when you felt embarrassed, when you did something you regretted. Holding regrets in your energy field is the same as holding grudges, only this time it's yourself that you need to forgive. You may identify certain periods in your life when you were going through a phase you later felt embarrassed about. Or something specific, like how you broke up with a boyfriend/ girlfriend or how you behaved when they broke up with you. Make that list, open the closet and take out all the skeletons. There's no point doing this if you only go halfway.

❖ Spend some time with your list, getting familiar with it. Check in with yourself and see if you're holding the energy still. You might think you are, but then realize you aren't feeling any emotion around these items at all. On the other hand, you may need to process the impact the list has on you – just how many things you haven't actually let go of. Or you may feel like congratulating yourself for not having many things. Truly, this depends on where you are on your life's journey.

❖ Once you have a final list of active issues that you are still working on, use different coloured pens to classify them into finished business and unfinished business.

Unfinished business can take longer to sort out, but it is worth doing. If you have unfinished business which still has a negative impact on your life, it's much better to be aware of it than not. You might need to cast your mind back to the event, drop down into your body and ask yourself (from your heart, not from your head), 'Is this really over or do I need to do something before I can let it go?' Perhaps what you need to do is forgive yourself, or contact someone and apologize to them. If the other person isn't ready to forgive you then you have to live with that, but you can expand your energy field so that they cannot open your closet and take out all the skeletons. The tie-cutting exercise (*see page 62*) can be useful in this type of circumstance. Do it as many times as you feel you need to.

Never get in touch with someone as part of this exercise to show grievance and demand an apology from them. This work is specifically to clear and raise your energy vibration, not to cause more problems in your life.

This part of the exercise has been about awareness, as your brain needs to know where you are with your forgiveness work. You will have already let go of some of the items on your list, but some of them you won't. Now you know what you're still holding on to, the second part of this exercise is the letting-go part. It's energetic, and done through visualization techniques. You don't have to do this all on the same day.

EXERCISE

Forgive Everyone: Part II

✦ Choose one issue from your list that you think you are ready to let go of completely. It can be either finished business or unfinished business. This is about how you are holding the issue in your energy field, so even if it's unfinished, there could still be a positive shift from trying this exercise.

✦ Sit in your quiet meditation space and make sure you're warm enough and won't fall asleep during this exercise. Drop down into your body and release all tension. Take your time with it.

✦ Check in with yourself and say:

'I give myself permission to forgive [name] because of [issue] and let go of the heavy energy I feel around it.' [This can include forgiving yourself, too.]

✦ Wait and let your body answer. Breathe out any fear or anxiety that may arise. If there's a lot of fear, you may not be ready to complete this exercise yet. Ask what the fear is about and let your body tell you. Close your eyes and let an image speak to you, a thought, a feeling, even a song. And don't push yourself. Find out what the block is, what the fear is, and then walk away from this exercise until you are ready to try again.

✦ If you get the okay to go ahead with it, you can set your intention to let the emotion go through a visualization. Allow your subconscious mind to show you an image of how you are now as you hold this heavy grudge energy in your energy field. Lack of forgiveness could appear as a messy bedroom, a field, a garden, a house, or it could be a beach after a storm, a cave with rocks strewn about. It could appear as you with daggers and glass sticking out of your body, or the other person looking the same way if you were the one inflicting the hurt. Ask if this is everything or if there is more and wait till the visualization settles and comes into balance and you know that you have the picture right.

❖ Now you can go to work. If it's a room that's messy, clean it up, put everything away or throw it away, burn what needs to be burned, open the windows to let the light and air in and paint the walls. If it's outside, perhaps stones need to be smashed or moved. Basically you're bringing order to chaos and releasing what you no longer need. If it's glass or daggers in a body, see yourself gently pulling them out and applying a poultice, bandages and healing ointment. See the wounds healing up and closing. Yes, there may be a scar, but it's not an open wound, and that's an improvement. Don't push this too far: your brain might want to see a fully healed person or a bright, clean, shiny room, but you might not get it all completed the first time around. Remember, *any improvement is a big improvement*. And the more you trust the process, the easier it gets. So, do as much as you can for now. Know that when you come back it will have shifted again, as you come into balance and alignment with the work in the physical world as well as in the energetic dimension.

❖ Breathe. Feel the changes in your energy field and feel the changes in your body from the work you have done. Know that by releasing grudges and resentments you are healing your physical body too, moving towards vibrant, radiant health and away from disease. It's big and important work you are doing. People have healed from serious illness by doing forgiveness work.

❖ When you're ready, give thanks. Ask if there is anything else you need to do. Then allow the images to dissolve and come back to the room.

You might have to repeat this part of the exercise several times before you really, truly let go of all the heavy emotion attached to the issue.

If you've been doing the work in the book up to now, you may value yourself more, understand yourself more and like yourself more than you did before you started. I hope you are also beginning to recognize the times in your life where you really did do the best you could with what you had.

Just like Sarah, you can learn to accept the fact that what you would do now, knowing what you know now, is different from what you did in the past. But you didn't know then what you know now, so you have to give yourself the benefit of the doubt. You wouldn't be reading this if you hadn't done what you did. All you've experienced, all you've been through, has led you to this present moment. Cherish it, all of it, good and bad. Cherish it all. Know that you are worthwhile. You deserve to be happy. (If you don't resonate with these sentiments as you read them, I suggest you go back to Chapter 3 and work through some of the exercises on self-worth again.)

Releasing All Your Secrets

Keeping secrets can block a substantial amount of your energy. You can be keeping a secret from yourself as well as from someone else. This is called 'being in denial'.

Imagine each secret is a beach ball and you're standing in the sea. To keep the secrets hidden, you need to push the beach balls under the water. The more balls you have to hide, the harder it gets for you, until one day something throws you off-balance and hey presto, all the beach balls come up to the surface and you're surrounded by them. Part of the drain on your energy when keeping a secret is the fear that this will happen.

By their very nature, secrets are complicated, and more common than you may think. Some have a much bigger impact on your life than others. These include the ones you keep from yourself, such as hating your job but not wanting to admit it to yourself because you need the money from it, or knowing that you no longer have anything in common with a partner or a friend but not wanting to have to go through a relationship break-up. You can also be in denial of falling out of love, falling in love, having an addiction, wanting to change (or drop) religious beliefs, being gay and/or having gender identity issues.

Secrets that you may be aware of but keep from other people may include bereavements such as having an abortion, having a baby and giving it away or losing a child. You might have mental health issues that you don't want the people at work to know about. Secret behaviour that you keep from other people can include shoplifting, drinking, gambling, taking drugs, embezzlement, eating disorders, physical violence and/or infidelity. This is all natural and I'm not judging you here at all. I just want you to learn about how you are organizing yourself (see how many beach balls you're trying to keep under the waves, so to speak), so you can do something about it if you feel you need to.

> **Know this: anything you do that you do not approve of creates heaviness in your energy field.**

You are aware of what you are doing both consciously and subconsciously. And by doing things that you don't approve of, you give yourself material to use against yourself in self-sabotage cycles. It creates low self-esteem and low self-worth, and it can possibly undo the good work that you have done from this book. (In the case of mental health issues, it's not the issue that creates the heaviness, it's the feeling that you have to keep it a secret that drains your energy.)

There are a few things that you can do with secrets, but the main thing for your wellness is to dissolve the heavy energy from your energy field so it becomes lighter and higher in vibration. You can consider getting professional help, telling someone you trust or doing some work on this yourself. Getting support from a professional can help you feel validated and over time may help you change unwanted behaviour into something healthier. Telling someone you trust can be a relief, as you no longer feel you're the only one carrying the weight of a burden. It's like having two pairs of hands holding those beach balls under the water instead of doing it all yourself. It can help to talk to someone because you will see that you aren't the only one with a secret. Life is still going on around you and it may feel easier to be in the world once this has been released.

When you dissolve a secret from your energy field using energy healing, you're dissolving how you're holding the energy of the secret. This works best for past events that don't have a direct impact on your life today, such as giving away a baby. If the secret you want to heal is unwanted behaviour, unless you put an end to the behaviour, this method is not one that will help you.

Talking about Secrets

Anorexia is an eating disorder that triggers unwanted behaviour. I once had a client who was anorexic. It started out as small thing and grew into a life-consuming issue and she ended up in hospital with it. When she came to see me, she was over the worst, back to a healthy weight and mostly okay. She found, however, that when life was getting complicated she resorted to stopping eating again so she felt that she had some sense of control over her world. She would pretend to eat in front of her family and in front of her boyfriend, and they thought that all was well. But when she realized she was beginning to lie to herself too, she decided she didn't want this to be a secret she kept from herself, so she came to see me to work through it and clear it. Admitting it to herself and knowing she was supported by me helped her to find new coping mechanisms and she was able to return to healthy eating patterns.

Having an addiction can also trigger unwanted behaviour, and the addict might not even realize that there's a problem. We all have addictive tendencies, but they aren't addictions unless they get out of hand. If behaviour related to gambling, drinking, substance abuse or even shopping, eating or sex *is* creating upset for you or anyone else in your life, though, it's possible that it is an addiction. If you have a problem with an addiction, please recognize that it can take over your life and drain your energy as well as the energy of those around you. To feel truly well, you need to face up to the difficult work of letting it go. Find someone who can support you, who can work with your mind, body and spirit to bring you to a new space of being. It can take a lot of energy to hide an addiction from your loved ones, so it might help if you tell your partner, your family or a loved one too.

Life is real, it can be hard, and we go through many different situations and do things that we sometimes regret. Whatever your secret(s) may be, it may ease the pain if you talk to someone. It might not be as bad as you think it is. Perhaps sharing it all with someone and having them accept you for who you are, secret(s) and all, will ease the blocks and the gates that you place on your flow of energy and you can open up more to life and move on. It is a risk, but as Anaïs Nin says, sometimes the risk of staying a bud is greater than the risk of opening up and becoming a flower.

Dissolving Secrets from Your Energy Field Yourself

Perhaps you have come to terms with your secrets over many years and they are no longer major blocks but things you have learned to live with. I'm a great believer in 'if it ain't broke, don't fix it'. However, if something is getting in the way of your living a clear and joyful life, you can check in with your essential self to see how it is impacting on you. Use the 'Clearing Out the River' exercise (*page 149*), with the intention of your river showing you how a secret is blocking your energy flow. Then breathe with the river and clear it out. Imagine the attention you are giving this is helping the blockages to be released and move on. Allow your body to open as the blockages are released.

Another way to do this is to visualize the beach balls you are holding under the water. Perhaps you could name them, thank them and then let them go.

Or, when you're in a relaxed state, you could simply ask your body to show you where you are holding emotional heaviness around something specific, then breathe through it and send love and gratitude to it. You will need your awareness to be in two places at once for this – with your imagination, but also in your physical body as you work. Keep your feet on the ground and breathe out anything that is loosened or dislodged or comes to the surface as you work in your mind's eye. Breathe it all out and let it flow into Mother Earth through your feet.

If you want more energy healing techniques that can help with this, there are many of them in my book *Energy Healing*.

Do your energy work a few times to come into balance. You might still want to get professional help or talk to a friend afterwards. If you're fully committed to being well, then you need to do the right thing. You deserve it.

Bringing the Magic Back

Sometimes healing deep inner wounds isn't about letting go but about inviting something in that was lost. Did you have your dreams pulled out from under your feet when you were small? What magical thing was it that you wanted to be that you weren't allowed to be? A singer? An actor?

An artist? Did a part of you shut down, shut off, switch off completely at some point in your life because you couldn't follow your soul's desire?

I once had a client who was told by her music teacher that she would never be a musician. She stopped playing the violin and fell into a depression until she took it back up in her fifties. Even though she knew at 50 that she would never play professionally, she found so much freedom in being able to express herself through her music that it opened up a door to let joy and happiness into her life.

Take some time to honour your dreams, to spend time with them. Do you even know what they are? Give yourself permission to be what you long to be. You may not make a living from it, but if you allow yourself to do it or be it, you may find that it is where you shine brightest. Be inspired – there are many late bloomers out there, such as Brian Dennehy, who didn't start his acting career until the age of 38, or Mary Wesley, whose first novel was published when she was 70, or Christopher Lee, who recorded his first heavy metal album when he was in his eighties!

Start by remembering what it was that you loved. Then say, 'I give myself permission to do what I love, no matter what anyone says about it.' Feel that you *can* do it – you're the adult now and the only one criticizing you is you. Say it out loud: 'I can and I will!'

Then, if you need new skills, get them. Invest in drawing lessons, buy yourself a saxophone or a new computer, get a voice coach – just save up and do it! You are worthwhile and you are beginning to feel your worth, so invest in yourself and show yourself you mean what you say. Remember it's much cheaper than paying doctors when you get sick from unhappiness. And invest the time you need to strengthen those muscles again. If you were going to run a marathon, you'd go into training first. Here, too, you need to build your strength up slowly.

Let your heart shine, open to the light and really receive the beauty and magical feeling that you experience when you are stepping into your natural talents. By releasing limiting beliefs around any skill or talent you may have and allowing yourself to truly, deeply experience it in its full beauty and power can bring magic back into your life.

Ceremonies to Release the Energy of Old Wounds

These are only some of the things that you can do to release deep, inner wounding. There is always more, and there are many ways to do the work. If we all liked vanilla ice cream, they'd not have invented chocolate or pistachio flavor!

When you've done deep healing work on the energetic plane, it's important to consolidate it with something in the physical world that will strengthen your awareness that you've finally let an issue go and started to heal. So this section is about making time for ceremony to mark the fact that you have let go of something big and important.

Ceremony marks an occasion – it's a specific action on a specific date and time. It makes an achievement real for you. Then, if you feel any old emotions surfacing relating to the issue in times to come, you can say to yourself, 'I let that go last 12 November. So this is either not my emotion and I've picked it up from someone else or it is something new.' Just knowing this can be empowering. It puts you in a position of power, rather than being a victim.

I offer you two ceremonies here, but you only need to do one to consolidate one issue. You can choose which one is appropriate for you depending on where you live and what is available to you. You can also adapt these ceremonies or create your own to honour your work. However you do this, the principles are the same: invoking the energies in your body, releasing them into a physical object and calling on the elements of nature to release them from the physical object and then from your body.

WATER CEREMONY

Try to do this ceremony outside. Water in motion, such as a river or a waterfall, is best. It won't work if the water is still or stagnant.

Go for a walk thinking of the particular issue that you are marking on this occasion. On your walk, gather sticks or stones to represent the people you've forgiven or the issues you've let go.

When you have all your sticks or stones ready, find a spot by the water where you feel safe to do this work. If you want, you can say:

> *'I now hold a ceremony of letting go. I ask the universe to create a safe space around me where I will not be disturbed until it is complete.'*

Depending on where you are on your journey, you can call in the four directions, spirit guides, power animals or angels, or just be quiet and peaceful, mindful in your body.

Think of the person you've forgiven or the issue you have moved on from. As you reflect on what has happened, allow any emotions left in your body to be stirred up and rise in you. Remember you're celebrating that you've moved on, so perhaps the emotions will be joy and gratitude instead of the familiar emotional pain. If there is any emotional pain remaining, raise a stick or stone to your lips and blow the emotions into it to let them go. Gently repeat this until you feel the energy shifting out your body and into the object. If you are feeling joy, you can also blow this into the stick or stone in gratitude, like a prayer.

Say to yourself:

'I let/have let this go completely. I give permission to let this go and move on with my life.'

If your object is a stick, you can break it in two to release the energy. Then throw your stick or stone into the water and watch it floating downstream. Feel your body relax and raise its vibration as it connects with nature. Know that the work is done and marked and finished with, and if any further thoughts arise in you, you can gently tell them, 'Thank you, but that has been released and you are no longer necessary.'

Note: If the feelings do come up again at a later date, it could either be another layer of the work revealing itself to you, or it could be that you've picked up similar energies from somewhere else and your body is interpreting them as the same issue.

FIRE CEREMONY

You can do this ceremony outside if you have somewhere to light a fire that is safe and legal. You can also do it inside your home in the fireplace or you can use a candle and a metal bucket, or a tea light and a plate. Be safe with fire; use your common sense.

Light the fire or candle and wait until you have a good flame to work with. Tune in to the energy of the fire so that it feels good to you and you are in balance with it.

Ask the fire if it will help you release the last of the heavy energies that you are carrying concerning this particular person or issue. Take a pen and a small piece of paper and write down the name of the person/issue that you are releasing. Fold the paper up small for burning and blow the feelings you are experiencing out of your body and into the paper. If you have a large fire to work with, you can use a stick instead of the paper and blow the issue into it just as you would in the water ceremony.

As the fire burns your issue, feel the energy leaving your body. Allow yourself to feel cleansed and healed.

Stay with it until the paper has turned to ash, the stick has turned to dust. Know that it is done, and if any old thoughts or emotions arise around this person or issue, just as before you can gently tell them that the work is done and they are no longer needed.

Healing is an Ongoing Process

If you are having trouble with any of these exercises, I have a suite of healing meditations and sessions available for download from my website. You might find it easier to work at a deeper level with closed eyes and the feeling of my energy around you. You can go to www.abby-wynne.com and see what you can find to help you on your journey of healing.

It is when you are healing your deep inner wounding that you are most likely to need extra support. You do know deep down in your heart that you won't be happy as long as you're holding grief, guilt, shame or fear. If you really want to be well, you have to recognize what is in you, take responsibility for it and do your work. I have an appendix at the back of this book with information on professional help, including your rights as a client. I also have a list of resources you may wish to draw on.

Even if you've just read through this chapter and haven't done any of the exercises, know that as you read it, a seed was being planted in your soul. When you're ready, the seed will blossom and you'll know what to do. And also know that you can let go of inner wounds just by giving yourself permission to heal.

Thank you for being here and for being you. You're doing great work, truly you are.

PART III

STAYING WELL

*Life constantly shifts and changes.
To stay well we need deliberate focus,
awareness and a proactive approach
to keep ourselves in balance.*

Chapter 6

Maintaining a Good Baseline Wellness Score

'Before enlightenment, chop wood, carry water.
After enlightenment, chop wood, carry water.'
ZEN PROVERB

'A harmonious person is never vibrating
at the same rate as a germ.'
FLORENCE SCOVEL SHINN

What a lot of work you've done to be here now, reading this chapter. I never said it was going to be easy! Please don't feel you've 'cheated' if you've skipped some of it, or feel you've not gone deeply enough with some of the exercises. This is your process and it's all here for you when you're ready, in your own time.

Perhaps some of you will never clean up your river completely, and that's okay. If you can see small improvements on your day-to-day wellness scale by doing small things for yourself, great! That's what it's all about. If you can't, you may need to take stronger action, so pick one thing and work on that. Just take it one piece at a time.

How to Stay Well

However well you feel now, remember that things happen on a day-to-day basis that can knock you sideways. You may be a spiritual essence in a physical body, but you live in a three-dimensional material world. Fortunately, as you go through the process of growth, life becomes less about what's happened to you and more about how you carry what's happened to you. As you learn to let go of the old stuff, you find it easier to let go of the new stuff too.

This chapter will help you learn how to maintain a high wellness level over time. What I offer here are some things to consider, but it's by no means a comprehensive list. You may feel you know some of it already, and there is only so much I can cover in one chapter. Looking after yourself is a hot topic in the health supplements in the newspapers, it's all over social media and none of it is unfamiliar. But how much of it are you actually taking on in your own life? Perhaps your attitude towards your health could change as you grow to like yourself more.

Staying well is a balance between growth, upgrading your life and good lifestyle practices. It's true that you may need to change how you are living your life in order to stay well for the rest of your life. If you raise the vibration of your energy, you will need to raise the vibration of how you are living to match it. That's what I mean by a lifestyle upgrade. My attitude is this: change one thing, but change it for *life*.

If you want to feel well, it's so important to treat yourself well *all the time* – not just for the two weeks a year you go on holiday. Wouldn't it be wonderful to feel rested, relatively stress-free and happy every day for the rest of your life? I don't believe short-term blasts of radical new behaviour are the recipe for lasting change. A lifestyle change means a change in the style of how you live your *life*, so take time to prepare for it and grow into the idea of it before you do it. And once you come into balance with that one thing, then you can try another thing. One step at a time.

This chapter looks at body, mind, emotions and soul all together to help you recognize what you would like to upgrade and maintain for each of these aspects. I'm giving you suggestions here; I'm not saying you have to do any of them. Sometimes it's very difficult to make changes like these, and some of them may not be appropriate for you, so be discerning. But don't say you don't have time. *You have to make the time to do the things that are important for your health.* And if you do decide to do something I suggest here, you may need to do some more research on it, perhaps by taking a class, looking it up on the internet or buying a book written by an expert.

If you do make the effort to create lifestyle changes, you might find that over time some of the bigger things that need to be cleared out of your river may clear by themselves as a result.

Looking After Your Body

If you're in pain or your body isn't in great shape, it's going to push down your baseline wellness score. Let's face it, you can spend a lot of energy just managing life if you're in physical pain most of the time. If you want to get well, you have to do something about it. Even if you've been diagnosed with something or are physically disabled, I'm pretty sure there still are some improvements you can make to your life situation that could bring you a little more relief than you're getting already. Do you know what they are?

Sometimes physical pain is caused by the emotional pain you're carrying in your body. At other times, though, there's a mechanical or chemical fault in the body that needs to be repaired and no amount of emotional work or energy healing is going to sort it out. If you need to go to a doctor, have you gone yet? Don't put it off, but don't feel that the doctor is the last-stop shop. You can make great improvements to the physical aspect of yourself just by changing what you eat and how you exercise.

I'm not an expert in nutrition, exercise or body chemistry, I'm just talking about using your common sense and looking after yourself. Yes, it does take effort, but you're probably more supported now that you've got energy healing working in the background, so you're carrying less emotional pain and have more energy available to put back into yourself. So, learn how to eat better if you are eating badly. Try to lose some weight if you feel you are an unhealthy weight. Make an effort to get fit if you're not fit. See a doctor if something is broken. If you want to be well, you have to invest the time and money into feeling better.

Food Is Fuel

You know what I'm going to say here! What you put into your body is what your body gets from you. We looked at the energy from thoughts and emotions earlier; food is also energy. If there isn't much of the good stuff in your food to absorb, your body goes without the nutrients it needs. The longer you go without, the more drained your body is. You're in charge of what you put into your body. Do you expect your body to be fully functional no matter how you treat it? It won't be.

Your body is running on empty if you eat too many processed foods, highly refined sugars and even too much wheat or corn. I've read that anything with an ingredient list isn't food. There are so many additives and preservatives these days that clog up and block our body. The best thing to be eating is fresh, high-quality, local seasonal food (or what your grandmother used to call *food*). Remember, if your gut is clogged up with toxins and is overloaded trying to digest heavily refined or processed food, it won't be clear to be effective when you want to check in with your gut instinct. Either it won't be able to communicate with you when you ask it a question or you won't be able to understand what it says, as it will speak to you with its proverbial mouth full of whatever you just ate!

Noticing what types of food you eat is a first step you could take, particularly if your choices shift and change depending on your mood. Notice, don't judge – remember it's about being nicer to yourself rather than finding more things to be upset about. But nevertheless, face it – if you want to have more of an awareness of your body, of how you're feeling, you need to look after it better. And you need to know what you're putting into your body, so you can alter it if necessary to get the best out of it.

At some level you are listening to your body and responding to its needs. But are you responding to your emotional body or to your physical body?

If you can get more in touch with your body, you will notice more and more when your emotional needs are overriding your physical needs. Be honest with yourself – remember, no more secrets. Do you really want to eat that large pizza or is the small pizza enough? If not, why not – what is it that you're really wanting to be filled up by? Ask your physical body what it wants. Maybe it actually wants a salad? Remember, your body is an aspect of you and it wants to do its best for you, but are you doing your best for it?

Reset Your Body

There is a case in standard psychology about a woman who was so disconnected from her physical needs that she didn't know when she was hungry anymore. She ate when her brain told her to eat, which was most of the time. Her doctor recommended that she fast for several days to reset her body. Fasting is something that you could consider doing if you are relatively healthy and not planning to do anything important for a few days. You need to drink water, but fasting can reset your system and water can help you flush out toxins that may have built up over time. I would only recommend this if it was something you wanted to do, though. Talk it over with your doctor or a health professional and plan to do it rather than jump right in and do it.

Make Small Changes

Perhaps all you need to do to get a better night's sleep is not eat cheese before you go to bed, cut down on snacking late at night or stop drinking anything with caffeine after 5 p.m. If you try all three at the same time, you won't know which one has made the difference, so try one thing at a time, see how you feel mentally, emotionally and physically, and then decide if it's a change you'd like to continue with.

Perhaps you feel you need to eat everything on your plate, so serving yourself a smaller portion or using smaller plates could be the small change that works best for you. Experiment, play, see how you go with it.

It's possible that changing what and how you eat is too big a job for you to manage yourself, so you may want to get some help. There are many ways to start looking at this. You could take an allergy test to see if there are foods to which you are intolerant (and I hate to say it, but if you're reading this book and are interested in energy work, there will be many foods to which you are intolerant, and they will probably be your favourite foods too). You could find a nutritionist, a food coach or even a therapist to help you work through your food issues. If you set your intention to find the right person to help you, they will appear – you'll read an article, you'll find a book, or you'll even hear about someone a friend of yours just saw who did remarkable work for them. Be open, listen to these signals and use your gut instinct to get a healthier gut.

Focus on Adding Healthier Food Rather Than Eliminating the Food You Love

There are two things that I would recommend you start thinking about cutting down on or cutting completely out of your diet: these are refined sugars and processed foods.

The way I approached doing this myself was initially to become aware of how much sugar there was in everything (it's shocking) and then to start adding lots of veggies to my diet in the form of green juices. That's right, I focused on *adding* juices to my diet, not on giving up sugar or anything else. Once I was adding more and more green juice to my diet, my cravings settled down and I found that I didn't want so much sugar or refined food. The other key part of this work was when I *did* eat sugary or processed food, I didn't get upset with myself about doing it. That made a massive difference to me. I began to trust that I could have whatever I wanted and I could relax with myself and with food. Over time, I was receiving more information about what my physical body wanted, rather than what my emotional body told me I needed. This took me two and a half years. In the last year or so before writing this book, I began to feel safe enough to let go of my emotional need for food.

Two and a half years to make a lifestyle change. That's the type of time I'm talking about for some of the changes in this chapter. They're a commitment and you need to switch on something deep inside you which says, 'Yes, I'm ready to do this.' Are you ready? You might need to think about it and come into balance with it for a while. That's part of the healing process too.

Weight Is a Spiritual and Emotional Issue

Are you hiding from the world because you are overweight? Or are you using your weight to hide from the world? Extra weight impacts your wellness scale because it's stopping you from enjoying life to the full. You may have children you'd like to get down on the floor and play with, but you're not comfortable doing it because you're overweight. You feel self-conscious when you walk in a public place; you hate not being able to buy the clothes you want. Carrying frustration and anger because of your physical body size means that at some level you are angry at your physical body. Your poor body! It's just there so that you can show up for life – it hasn't done anything wrong to you. Stop and think about what you are doing – why are you eating more than you need?

Many people use food to fill up a gaping inner emptiness that is craving to be filled – but not with food. With fulfilment, with love, with creativity, with fun, acceptance, forgiveness! We crave love, we crave spiritual connection – connection to something that's bigger than us. And if we don't know how to get that, the next best thing may be chocolate.

If weight is an issue for you, you do need to take some time to look at why you may be piling on the pounds. Don't be afraid of it. I've already said that secrets soak up too much energy – perhaps you're afraid of love or afraid of being hurt and so don't want to feel attractive. This is a secret you may be keeping from yourself. So, try my exercise for mindful eating (below). Ask for help if you need to. Remember that this isn't really about losing weight, it's about feeling well. Stop weighing yourself and concentrate on treating yourself better. The weight will fall off when you start to feel more comfortable in yourself. Then you just won't want to treat yourself badly anymore.

Exercise

Mindful Eating

❖ Take a few minutes to come into your body before you eat. Breathe in light and peace, breathe out stress. Breathe in light, breathe out anger and fear. Breathe in light, breathe out anxiety.

❖ Now ask your body what it would like to eat.

❖ Allow an image come into your mind. You may not have all the ingredients, but as you do this exercise more regularly, you will become more prepared.

❖ If your body is choosing highly processed sugary foods, ask it if it would prefer something more natural, something healthier. If it says, 'No,' ask why, and wait for the response. 'I'm not feeling so good today' is usually what it says in this situation. So ask if this is an emotional need or a physical need. Maybe you need to rest, maybe you need to phone someone or do an energy-clearing exercise. Don't be upset if you can't shift the craving. Agree to work with your body and only eat as much as it needs.

❖ If what your body wants is healthy and you are in alignment with it, then prepare the food in a mindful, thoughtful way, being as present as you can to the preparation. This means not thinking about things that are going to happen tomorrow or what you're going to do after you eat. Stay with the food, with the cutting of the food, the cooking, the smells… Savour each spice you use. Give thanks for the food that is gifted to you.

❖ When you eat, eat slowly. Taste each mouthful and breathe slowly and evenly. Ask your stomach to tell you when it has had enough.

Exercise Is Good for Your Body

There are so many forms of exercise out there that if you don't like exercise perhaps you just haven't found what gives you pleasure yet. Seriously! Some people like tai chi, while others prefer yoga. Some like swimming, others like walking. What do you like to do? I like the gym, free weights, walking and yoga. I don't enjoy swimming and I can't get the hang of tai chi, so I don't push myself to do those things. Why suffer? Choose activities that you enjoy. Going to boot camp may look great on TV, but if you hate every minute of it, you'll be suffering more than you already are.

Whatever you do, build it up slowly. You could start with an app, an online class or a drop-in class. Perhaps buddying up with someone to work with would increase your motivation? You need to make the time to exercise, so increase its importance in your mind. You can also be creative here. If, for example, your sister is complaining you don't spend enough time with her and you say you don't have enough time to exercise, perhaps you could meet her at the local Zumba class and grab a juice afterwards?

Looking After Your Mind

Just as what you put into your body and how you work it are important for your wellness, so are what you put into your mind and how you work that too.

Watch What You Say

Words are more powerful than you think. You have seen how powerful they can be when used in affirmations. If in your ordinary day-to-day speech you constantly use words that are of a low vibration, you can bring yourself down to that low vibration. I had a friend who called herself stupid all the time. That had to hurt.

Become aware of the words you use most of the time and see if you can make some improvements. Are you ranting about the bus being late, the television programming being bad, the state of the economy being dire? Do you need to spend so much time complaining? Notice how much energy you're spending on recognizing the negative in your life and perhaps start to recognize the positive instead. There's not much difference in spelling between 'complaint' and 'compliment' – see if you can turn things around and begin to talk more about the good things that have happened to you than the bad.

Isn't it funny, though, how people are more interested when bad things happen to other people? It seems to be a natural response. The key thought behind it is: *Thank goodness it didn't happen to me.* Take a day specially to notice when you are doing this. Or when you are being judgemental or gossiping about other people. Or complaining, or joining in when someone else is complaining. What's the first thing that comes out of your mouth when someone gives you the wrong change at the supermarket or cuts in front of you on the road? Are you being the loving person that you wish to be? What would you hope that someone would say if you were the one to make the mistake?

Honestly, this is a very difficult thing to keep track of, but keep track of it you must. At the very least, when you say hurtful things about someone behind their back, try to not send the energy of hurt out there with the words. Let that combust in your mind instead and bring yourself back to a loving, open heart.

One more thing on watching what you say: turning a negative statement into a positive one changes its vibration. What do you feel when you say 'the fight against cancer' as opposed to saying 'research for vibrant health'? Are they the same thing? What else can you turn into a positive? Try to do this more often and see what happens.

Watch What You Watch/Listen to

I just turned off the news one day and really enjoyed the blissful peace I received instead. There's a difference between knowing what's going on in the world and immersing yourself in a constant flow of bad news. This goes for television shows too – don't just sit there mindlessly and watch whatever's coming on next, deliberately choose things you're interested in. Listen to music that uplifts you. Avoid things that upset you. You deserve to be happy, not to go to bed terrified because you watched a horror movie you really didn't enjoy. There's enough horror out there, you don't need to feed yourself more of it.

Problem is, once you start being aware of this, you may have trouble being around people who are constantly negative. This can and probably will impact upon some of your friendships. If they're worth the effort, you can have a conversation about it and see where it goes from there.

Looking After Your Emotional Health

Being clear about the difference between self-care and selfishness is vital when it comes to looking after your emotional health. If you're not sure, maybe have a conversation with a friend or do some research or work on the concepts at a deeper level so you can embrace the work of looking after yourself without feeling guilty. And of course self-care is directly tied into self-worth, so if you're having trouble with this, revisit the work in Chapter 3.

Saying 'No'

People don't like to hear 'no' and we're afraid to say it, perhaps because we've had a 'no' said to us that hurt. So we skirt around saying 'no', and in doing so, we give away parts of ourselves, sometimes too many parts, which drains us and leaves us vulnerable.

Always check in with your wellness scale before saying 'yes', because saying 'yes' to someone else could be saying 'no' to yourself. Of course if it's an emergency, you will do the best you can, but be discerning – is it a genuine emergency or is it someone's perceived emergency? (Remember what I said about urgency in Chapter 4? Slow it all down and take a wellness reading before you respond.)

There are ways that you can say 'no' that don't hurt as much as a blatant 'no'. For example, if your needy but fun friend wants to meet you for a chat and your wellness scale is at 4, tell her you're not able to meet her today, could you make it another time? This is putting it off rather than saying 'no' to her. The phrase 'I'm not able to' is not something that is hurtful, and you're not lying either. 'I'm not up for a visit today' is another way you could say it if you need to. Stand your ground. If she really, really has something she wants to share with you, chances are she's in a needy space, so all the more reason for you to say 'no'!

Saying 'no' and meaning 'no' with confidence comes over time. To help in the meantime, you might like to revisit the power statements in Chapter 4 (*see page 110*), or write some of your own.

Take Time for Yourself

If you're upset you have to give yourself the time to experience that. Be with the emotions rather than running from them. Breathe with them. Know they will pass. Be patient with yourself. You might not even know why you're feeling bad and making space will give you the time to think things through. The worst thing you can do when you're feeling emotional is put pressure on yourself to stop feeling that way. Truly. Just sitting with yourself and acknowledging that you're not happy can really help. Without even having to know why. Try this exercise:

EXERCISE

Be Gentle with Yourself

Sit in a chair in a quiet room and breathe. Slow down. Go inwards and connect to your heart as best as you can. Breathe with your heart and speak to it lovingly, saying things like:

- ❖ 'I know things are difficult right now.'
- ❖ 'I see you.'
- ❖ 'It's okay to feel this way.'
- ❖ 'I give permission to feel these emotions.'
- ❖ 'I let these emotions pass through me.'
- ❖ 'I am here, behind these emotions.'
- ❖ 'These emotions are not me. I can feel them. I let them pass through me.'

Don't jump up too quickly from doing this. Stay with it and let the emotions pass. If you want to, ground yourself and let your emotions flow through your body and into the ground.

If this is too difficult, you can play some healing music and just sit with your heart and breathe with it. It's good to discover what music you like and have a playlist ready for times like this. Classical music can be great (especially Bach, Mozart or Beethoven), or you could get some meditative music or Indian classical flute music. Some of my friends like to play electronica, alternative music, jazz or blues to lift themselves out of heavy clouds of emotional energy. Discover what feels right for you.

❈ ❈ ❈ ❈

Dealing with Unexpected Stress

Things happen in this life, and not all of them are pleasant. The car breaks down when we're already late for work, our physical body breaks down, or someone else's body breaks down and our routine is disrupted to deal with the fall-out from it.

I believe that we are creatures of habit, so anything that throws us out of our routine can be a source of stress. Most of us like to know what we're going to be doing, where and with whom most of the time. We like to be able to plan the day – what to wear, what to take with us, and so on. We want to make sure our phone is charged. Little things like that seem very important. I know people who become incredibly stressed if their phone runs out of battery – not that they need to call anyone, but their mindset is that having a fully charged phone all the time is a necessity. But logically, is it really? We can manage on a nearly dead phone battery if we don't have to call anyone. It's our anticipation that we'll need to call someone that creates the stress. So a relatively small thing such as a nearly dead phone can be a trigger for a lot of stress if we let it.

> *My client doesn't like living alone, as she is afraid that things will break. We discuss what happened the last time things broke in her house.*
>
> *'Well, the tap wouldn't turn off. That was very scary. The sink overflowed and there was water everywhere.'*
>
> *'What did you do?'*
>
> *'I called the plumber and he came within the hour. He did a great job and fixed the sink and helped me mop up the mess.'*

'How did you feel once it was all sorted out?'

'Better. But the same week the house alarm went off and it wouldn't stop. I had to phone the alarm people to get them to fix it.'

'But look, you were able to do it and they came and they fixed it?'

'Yes, they did. But I was very upset about it. I didn't know who to call and it took me an hour just to get through to the right person.'

'I'd imagine you were upset by that,' I say. 'It's not pleasant listening to an alarm, especially if it's your own. What if you and I make a list of all the things that have broken in your house and all the things that haven't broken yet, and then when you go home you can look up all the names of the people who will help you fix them in an emergency? That way you'll have a list ready for the next time.'

'That could really help. Actually that's a very good idea.'

Anything that reduces stress in an unexpected situation is very helpful. A car breaking down or a tap not turning off isn't much fun, but there are things that are much worse than those. How do you manage then? Pull back, ground and centre yourself. Remember the important things. Orient yourself to the situation, what is happening, what needs to be done. It sounds straightforward, but it isn't if fear and panic take over and cloud your thoughts. You can't do anything when you panic and you make bad decisions when you act out of fear. Instead, feel your feet on the ground and, if it helps, ask the universe to help you stay focused and to send the best help available your way. Know who you can call to help you as you deal with the situation, and ask them to help you without fear. Remember, if it was the other way round, you'd be right over there helping them. Know you are valued and worthwhile and that you have just as much right to ask for help as anyone else.

Looking After Your Soul

So often the soul is forgotten in our self-care activities. We cannot afford to neglect it anymore. Factor in looking after your spiritual essence as part of a routine that is non-negotiable and I guarantee you'll feel much happier in your day-to-day life.

Having a Daily Spiritual Practice

One of the first questions I ask clients is this: 'Do you have a daily spiritual practice?' By this I mean: 'Do you do something every day to disconnect from the craziness around you and reconnect to yourself?' Connecting to your emotional body and your physical body, letting go of the urgency of your thoughts and grounding yourself to the Earth puts everything back into perspective.

> *If you want to live a wholehearted life, a life that*
> *you love, you need a daily spiritual practice.*

If you don't have a daily spiritual practice, you will shift back into old patterns of disconnection, start to feel resentment and anger, be intolerant and slide back into victim mentality. You've already done the work to come out of this way of thinking and you deserve to stay this way.

Be honest with yourself and notice what your tendencies are when you start to disconnect from your essential self. Do you get snappy? Overtired? Do you lose motivation for life? Feel more emotional? It's different for everyone, and by getting to know yourself you can see the warning signs and know when something needs to be done.

Your spiritual practice can be anything that brings you closer to your heart and soul. You can vary it too, if you like. Here are some things the people from my Facebook page say they do as their spiritual practice:

> *Mindfulness meditation, yoga, walking meditation, saying 'thank you' three times in the morning, grounding and breathing exercises, sitting under a tree, listening to specific music tracks, breathing meditation, praying, colouring, painting, singing, having a coffee ritual, going to the ocean, daily contemplation and gratitude, Vipassana meditation, seeing life through the eyes of a dog, spending time with horses, going to church, speaking out loud to God, energy healing, tai chi, ecstatic dance, cooking with love, playing a musical instrument...*

I love the variation. There are so many different types of people and there are so many different types of spiritual practice, and they are all valid. Going to church and praying can be a spiritual experience. And seeing life through the eyes of a dog – what a wonderful idea! I asked about that and the woman said, 'Dogs are pure compassion, as are horses and other animals.' Now you can see where she's coming from!

Switching Off Your Phone

People nowadays are connected to their phones. They see them as an extension of themselves. There's actually a condition called 'cell phone separation anxiety', in which people get highly agitated and anxious if they can't find their phone. And 'nomophobia' is the fear of being unreachable by phone. It's becoming apparent that the generations who have grown up with smartphones and tablets are so immersed in their phones they can't tell the difference between being online and offline. They are online *all the time*.

Here's a test: have you ever put your phone on silent and become occupied doing something, then had an urge to check it, only to find a meaningful message waiting for you? It was almost as if you just knew that it was there. Instances like this occur because you're connected to the energy of your phone in a dual flow: you flow out and it flows in, it flows in and you flow out – whether your brain is aware of it or not. What are you allowing into your energy field? What are you putting out there?

Connection to a computer network, whether it's the telephone network or the internet or both, affects your energy field. It also can affect how you hold your boundaries and your personal space. For example, your Facebook timeline becomes your personal space and if someone posts a photo or news article on it that you don't like, you can feel as angry as if someone had trespassed on your property. Amazing, isn't it? Facebook friends can connect to your energy and drain you just as other friends can (we looked at this in Chapter 3). Do be careful to whom you connect and how much of yourself you give away online.

And remember, once that embarrassing photo of you is up there, it's up there for ever. Even if you change your mind and take it down, third-party websites won't always delete it from their servers, as that would take up valuable administration time, and you don't know how many people have already downloaded it to their own computer or taken a screengrab of it in the meantime. This is the same energetically as giving your power away to the internet and the people you are connected to.

It doesn't have to be this way – you can take your power back from the internet by using it as the focus for the 'Reclaiming Your Power and Strength' exercise (see page 116). See the internet as fun, not as a part of you. Disconnect from it (and your phone) energetically on a regular basis as well as being aware of when you are online and when you are offline.

How do you do this? Simple! Switch it off. Energetically, switching your phone off is a completely different experience from switching it to silent. On silent, it's still connected to the network, still active. It ticks away in the background, connecting to the network every so often, and if it's a smartphone loaded up with apps, the apps work away in the background, dipping in and out of the internet without you even knowing. Your phone may be sitting silently on the floor beside you, but it's a singing, dancing, energetic party going on, with or without you.

Disconnect from your phone in stages and see what that feels like to you. You might be surprised. I was. One day I was out and about, but I decided to switch off email and the internet. I turned my phone into a phone! Wow, it felt different, I felt freer, more at peace. There wasn't so much going on in the background. It was as if a noisy washing-machine that was always there had just switched itself off. There was a gap. Peacefulness. Ahhh. Disconnection. And I've also turned off automatic fetch for my emails, so that I only get my emails when I want to get them, instead of them being pushed into my phone whenever they are sent to me. That makes a big difference too.

As a spiritual practice, turn your phone off for a certain amount of time every day. Drop completely off the radar. Create a sacred quiet space for yourself. That could be all you need to do. It could be as simple as that!

Checking in with Yourself

Checking in regularly with yourself using the wellness scale is a spiritual practice. Yes, it's true! Depending on how deep you go into your body, you can learn a lot of things from checking in.

Try this exercise now and see how you feel afterwards.

EXERCISE

Checking in as a Spiritual Practice

✦ Ask yourself how you are feeling. The first answer will come from your brain.

- Now breathe. Uncross your legs and feel your feet on the floor. Breathe. Allow your shoulders to settle as you read these words and open your chest.

- Breathe and breathe again. Enter your body more fully.

- Move your awareness down into your stomach and soften it, let it flop out – nobody is watching!

- Breathe in and out. Relax.

- Breathe in and out. Release any tension in your body through your limbs to the floor.

- Now take one more breath.

- Ask yourself again how you are feeling. Now you can feel into the true answer.

- At this level of connection you can ask if your body needs anything from you. What does your heart need? Your soul? Can you make a commitment to give it to yourself?

- Give thanks for the connection and gently bring your awareness back to the physical world around you.

Meditation

Meditation can be a scary word. It can sound as though you suddenly have to stop thinking. But you don't. There are many types of meditation. I find mindfulness meditation the most useful for busy people. Our brain is made to think, so with mindfulness we just need to be more aware of what we're thinking or have some control over what we're thinking rather than letting our thinking control us. Some of the exercises in this book are similar to mindful meditations, where you are focusing in the moment on doing something specific. So you've already done some meditation without even realizing it. Perhaps you've even enjoyed it, or enjoyed the sensation that you experienced after doing it.

Meditating allows you to slow down, disconnect from the world and be more present in the now, in your body. If you want to meditate as a spiritual practice, be open to trying a few different kinds to find out which one works best for you. Meditate for a short time to begin with and work your way up to a longer period which can easily fit into your lifestyle. Don't have aspirations to do 20 or 30 minutes of meditation a day if that's just not going to be practical for you. The worst thing you can do for yourself is make a commitment do to that and then not be able to do it and then be mean to yourself for letting yourself down. And you might not get to do it every day either. But a short meditation is better than none and as you feel the benefits you'll tend to meditate more often than not.

Here are a few different types of meditation to get you started. You will usually need a quiet space to try these out and your phone is best switched off.

BREATH MEDITATION

This is simply focusing on your breath going in and going out of your body and not getting caught up in your thoughts. You can notice the temperature of your breath as it leaves your body and the difference between breathing through your nose and your mouth. You can breathe normally or breathe while counting. You can try the following breathing exercises, repeating them several times to build up to at least five minutes of meditation. If you notice your mind wandering at any time, just bring your awareness gently back to your breath.

❖ Breathe in for a count of five, hold for a count of five, breathe out for a count of five.

❖ Breathe in for a count of five, breathe out for a count of five and then breathe in again for a count of five as a circular breath – no time out between breaths!

❖ Breathe in for a count of four, hold for a count of two, breathe out for a count of four, hold for a count of two.

My second youngest daughter loves the counting meditations as they help her settle down for a night's sleep. She does them in bed and she relaxes her body and drifts away to the counting. If you want to do this meditation in the middle of the day, don't do it lying down.

FOCUSED MEDITATION

This type of meditation invites you to focus on a sound, music or an affirmation or mantra. If you focus on music, really concentrate on the music, note by note, sound by sound, and forget your thoughts. When you focus on an affirmation or a mantra, feel the energy behind the words and allow it to become you. Prayer can be like a focused meditation when you become connected to the words, to the energy of the prayer taking you away from your thoughts.

Here are some sample mantras you could try:

- 'I am opening to love.'
- 'I am a channel for healing and love.'
- 'I am the light.'
- 'I'm sorry, please forgive me, thank you, I love you.'
- 'I give permission to let go of my emotional pain.'
- 'I am supported and loved.'
- 'I deserve to be happy.'

MINDFULNESS MEDITATION

In this type of meditation you just notice the sounds, the movements, anything that's going on around you right now. You don't have to be in a quiet and peaceful place to do this, just bring your awareness completely into the present moment. Feel what you are touching, appreciate what you are seeing.

As well as being still and mindful in a meditative space, you can also bring mindfulness meditation into the following activities, truly experiencing them in their fullness, as if for the first time:

- washing the dishes/cleaning the house
- walking in nature
- cooking and eating food
- playing music
- painting

- doing something intricate like a jigsaw puzzle
- colouring in a colouring book
- whatever else you like to do!

You do need to make sure you don't get triggered into remembering things that happened or thinking about things that are going to happen. Always 'be here now'. It takes practice.

MOVEMENT MEDITATION

This is using gentle motion of the body as a focus, rather than your thoughts. Make sure you have plenty of space to move around for this type of meditation. Movement meditation can include:

- gentle swaying or moving in circles, with or without music. You could allow yourself 'become the music' instead of being your thoughts.
- tai chi, qigong or other forms of martial art which require intense concentration
- yoga, dance – anything with a set practice that you can focus on instead of your thoughts
- walking meditation – focusing only on your footsteps, not your thoughts, counting each step up to 10, then starting again.

✳✳✳✳

Remember the purpose of meditation is to control your thoughts. You can take a yoga class after work and think about your dinner, write your to-do list in your head and go through a conversation you had with your mother while your body goes through the motions of yoga, but you won't get the benefit of a deep spiritual connection with yourself if you do it like this. Remind yourself that you have plenty of time after class to think about that stuff and this class is an opportunity to reconnect to yourself.

GUIDED MEDITATION

This is when you 'go on a journey' in a meditative space. Some of the exercises in this book are in the form of guided meditations, where you go to a landscape in your mind, do some work and then come back. These are also known as shamanic journeys. There are many types of guided meditation CDs available and many different people on different levels of their spiritual path who offer them. I recommend you listen to a guided meditation for the first time in a conscious state so you know what to expect and can feel comfortable when you relax and go deep with it. I find that there's nothing worse than relaxing into a guided meditation only to have the narrator take you somewhere that elicits fear or pain and jerks you back to reality again – it can feel like a shock to the system. Look after yourself and don't hand over your power to a guided meditation until you are fully confident that it is one that you resonate with.

It's possible to get bored with the same meditations, so mix them up. If, on the other hand, you love a particular meditation, stay with it for as long as it is working for you. Remember, you don't have to do a completely mind-clearing 'think of nothing' meditation – as powerful as that can be, most of us have trouble doing that. Active meditations give your mind something to do and take the focus off whatever's going on for you. And by changing where your attention is going, you can feel a lot better for the rest. I have several meditations for download on my website if you want to try them out.

Having an Energy-Healing Practice

Energy healing is a wonderful self-practice that you can incorporate into your day. To me, energy healing is shifting out of the old, slow, heavy energies and bringing in new, faster, lighter ones. You can combine it with meditation or do it on its own. If you want to use some the work from this book as a daily energy-healing practice, you can flip back to:

- ✹ Getting Clear of Other People's Energy (*page 46*)

- ✹ Calling Your Own Energies Back (*page 49*)

- ✹ Calling Your Energies Back from Specific Moments in Time (*page 52*)

- ✹ Cutting Ties in a Relationship (*page 62*)

- ✹ In Gratitude for My Body…' (*page 76*)

- ✹ Grounding, Part I (*page 82*)

✳ Using Energy Healing to Increase Your Self-Worth (*page 99*)

These are all exercises you could work with on a daily basis. If you wished, you could combine them, then close them off with an affirmation to raise your vibration.

If you've attended a workshop and have been attuned to a particular healing modality such as Reiki, allow yourself 10–20 minutes each day to do some self-healing. If you haven't been to a workshop, don't worry – energy healing is for everyone and you've already done some amazing energy-healing meditations here in this book. I have written two other books on healing, *Energy Healing for Everyone: A Practical Guide for Self-Healing* and *Energy Healing: Unlock Your Potential as a Healer and Bring Healing into Your Everyday Life*. Both of them teach you how to pull down high-vibrational energies to heal all aspects of yourself and how to bring healing into your life as a daily practice. No workshop or certification is needed to begin a daily practice of self-healing.

Expressing Your Essential Self Through Creativity

Creativity, too, can be a spiritual practice. It doesn't matter what you're creating – art, music, sculpture, writing, even a good meal. It's all about your intention and the energy you're holding while you're doing it. By connecting deeply with the work, textures, smells, colours, etc, and disconnecting from emotional pain, worries and fears, you transform the moment into something beautiful and rich.

This also includes playing a musical instrument, singing – anything at all that pulls you away from your thoughts and plunges you into a sea of possibilities, lights up your inner spark, gets your juices flowing and reconnects you to your joy. Knitting, sewing, scrapbooking, photography and/ or even creating a computer program could be vehicles for this type of experience. It might not be possible to be creative to this depth every day, but if you take a moment or two before you begin to disconnect from your thoughts, from other people or from your emotional pain, you can feed your soul and feel refreshed afterwards.

Emergency Self-Care

This chapter has been about upgrading your lifestyle and maintaining it, but sometimes you will slip below your baseline wellness level and you need to know two things: i) how you react when you slip downwards and ii) what you can do to help yourself come back up again.

I say to clients, 'If you're at 6–9, you're good, if you're at 3–5, you're okay, and if you're below 3, you may need some help.' You have less energy if you're below 3 and are less likely to invest energy in helping yourself, so a list of what works for you when you're down there is a really useful thing to have, because when you're actually there, you may not feel like doing anything at all.

> *The lower you are on your wellness scale, the less*
> *energy you are likely to spend on getting well.*

Take some time right now to make a list of things that you can do when you are below 3 on the wellness scale to get you back up to 4–5. These could be:

- calling a friend and talking about it

- going for a walk/swimming/dancing/yoga

- watching your favourite movie

- reading a good book

- sleeping

- having a bodywork session (energy healing/massage/reflexology)

- having a pampering session (manicure/hair/shopping)

- getting professional help to make sense of what's going on (psychotherapy/counselling/doctor)

Everyone's different and if there's nothing on this list that you think would help you, then write your own list. This work is *your* work and there's no point pretending something's good when it doesn't make you feel better at all. Perhaps bowling, painting, knitting, karaoke or horse-riding are more your style. Spending time with animals or in nature doesn't take too much energy and you can get quite a lot out of it. The need might never arise, but it's good to be prepared.

To Stay Well, You Must Treat Yourself Well

If you want to stay well, you have to treat yourself well. You have to be nicer to yourself than you ever were before you picked up this book. You are more aware of all the aspects of yourself now. You have to look after all of them – that way they'll look after you, too.

Treat your body as your best friend, as a part of you that loves you and would do anything for you.

Your body isn't you, remember, it's *a part* of you. If you think of it like that and start treating it better, it will perform better, stay healthier and be a wonderful resource for you. You know what you need to do for your body now, so make those changes slowly and let them stick with you for the rest of your life.

Treat your emotions as real, valid and important and give yourself the time to experience them and process them.

Emotions move slowly and need to be given attention. You'll still have days when you're emotional, so honour that aspect of yourself and give yourself the space you need.

Treat your mind as a helpful guide in your life, but don't hand it total control and let it make all the decisions.

Your brain, your ego, needs to know that it's a valid and important part of you, but there are other parts too, and all the aspects need to come together and work as a team for a fuller experience of life.

Treat your soul as an important part of you that also needs attention. It is the glue that holds all the aspects of you together.

Know that your soul longs to express itself through you in a creative way and that to be happy you need to make the time for it to do that.

And, above all else, believe that you deserve to be happy and you are lovable just because you exist. Stop feeling guilty about saying 'yes' to yourself. Learn to follow your joy. That's why you are here.

Chapter 7

Reaching Your Full Potential

'If one advances confidently in the direction of his dreams, and endeavors to live the life which he has imagined, he will meet with a success unexpected in common hours.'
HENRY DAVID THOREAU

'Don't die with your music still inside you.'
WAYNE DYER

Life doesn't just happen around you; you make choices every minute as to what you do, where you do it and whom you do it with. It's time for you to bring more of your awareness into the choices you're making so you can really live to your full potential.

I've given you lots of small and not-so-small things to do in this book that will enhance your happiness levels and improve your baseline wellness score, but you might need to make bigger life changes to become truly happy. These can be difficult, but they don't have to be impossible.

Know that the three most important things you need to be at peace with before you can be truly happy are:

- ✳ **where** you live

- ✳ **what** you do

- ✳ **who** you're with

Take a minute and ask yourself where you are with these. You won't be well if you do all the things in this book and are still battling with a life partner, going in every day to job you hate or living in a place that isn't a fit for your soul.

You may only need to make small changes to achieve great improvements, for example:

- ✳ Perhaps your partner is the right person but the relationship needs work. It's worth taking the time to sit down together and talk about it.

- ✳ Maybe the job you have is actually something you love but the company you work for isn't in line with your fundamental values.

- ✳ Maybe you live in the wrong part of town, long for a view of the mountains or the beach, or want a garden. Sometimes moving house is enough.

By doing the work in this book you have reclaimed your energy, created stronger boundaries and released the emotional weight that has been holding you back. This is your one and only life in this physical body and you deserve to be the happiest you can be. So, if moving to a new place, getting a new job or finding a new partner are things you know deep in your heart and soul you need to do, you might need to consider them at a practical level.

Figuring out what you want isn't always easy. It can be really confusing. It starts with learning who you are now, as a healthy and well person.

Who Are You Now? Releasing Your Old Identity

'I've been depressed for 20 years. It's a hard road. There have been days when I just couldn't do anything – weeks even. I had no friends, no life. Sometimes I wanted it all to end. Things have got better in the last two to three years, but being depressed makes things more difficult than they have to be.'

Patrick slumps in his chair and looks at his feet. He has been coming to see me for two years now and I know he is in a very different place from the one he was in when he first came.

'What would it be like if you woke up some days happy, other days a bit down, but most days okay?' I ask.

'That's kind of what it's like now, actually...'

'That's how most people are. What if you were no longer depressed?' I ask.

He sits up straight, with a concerned look. 'Then who would I be instead?'

'You'd still be Patrick,' I say, 'just not "Patrick with depression" anymore. How about just being Patrick?'

He takes some time to think, then says, 'There is a freedom in that all right, but it feels scary to me.'

Patrick's ego knows how to play the role of 'Depressed Patrick' and has been playing it for 20 years. It's not necessarily a happy role, but it's familiar. 'Happy Patrick' is new, it's a leap of faith. It's easier to stay with 'Depressed Patrick', because the ego knows that role so well. But the easy road isn't always the road to being well.

You know now that we are not what we feel, what we do or how we behave. Our essential selves lie beneath all of that. Our ego, however, finds it very comforting to attach itself to a label because then it knows what to do and knows its place in the world. It's like being given a role in a play with a script, a list of moods and possible outcomes. We may not like the role we've been given, but the ego understands it, grabs it and plays it with relish, because it wants to show us how good it is at playing that role. Depression as a diagnosis, or as a label we put on ourselves, has an energy, and a person who has been diagnosed with depression subconsciously knows the role they can play.

So a label makes our ego feel comforted and secure, even if it makes us ill. There are other benefits to labels too. They can be used as excuses to avoid things or to opt out of being responsible for our life. They can be great to fall back on as excuses for failing at something instead of getting up and trying again. They are opt-out clauses when it comes to putting in the work.

I'm certainly not making light of this: it is a very serious issue. Energetically, if you accept and take on a label, what you are doing is giving your permission and using your intention to become that label. You feed the label your power, your life-force, and over time as you surrender more to it, it becomes who you are and the essential you gets lost. Once you realize what you're doing, however, you can start to pull your energy away from the label and back into yourself. Then you can use that energy to get well.

Do you have a label that you don't even know you're carrying? Where do labels come from anyway? Let's take a deeper look at this now.

Where Labels Come from

Labels Come from Doctors

Doctors diagnose so they can create a treatment plan, but in diagnosing us they also label us, and if our ego is agreeable, it colludes with the diagnosis to create that state of being within us. We don't always create our illness, but we can empower it by taking on the energy of the diagnosis and letting it take over our life.

It's difficult not to hand your power over to doctors, or a team of doctors, as they are authority figures, particularly if they tell you have something life-threatening and that they can save your life. But a surgeon heals by doing surgery – that's what they do. So of course they will recommend surgery if they think they can help you. Start to see that a diagnosis is a transient thing that isn't an aspect of you but an aid to a doctor to help them prescribe your treatment. There are alternatives, and by being open to the possibility of other types of help, we step away from the energy of the diagnosis and back into the energy of who we are.

Remember: You are not your illness.

We are living in a world where there is an imbalance of power and most of us see doctors as much more powerful than we are. But we are becoming more empowered now as more alternative treatments are becoming available. If a doctor had diagnosed you with a particular disease or disorder before the year 2000 or so, culturally you wouldn't have questioned it and you would have taken it on as a large and weighty truth. What would have followed would have been a grieving process where you'd have surrendered your idea of who you were to the illness. Your ego would then have taken hold of this role and acted it out beautifully, and your body would have followed because it was expected of it. You would have become a person suffering from that particular illness. For example, you would have become a cancer patient, or someone fighting cancer, instead of being someone who had had many experiences in their life, including cancer. The wonderful thing is that this is changing now and doctors are being seen as one option of many as regards healing help. Knowing this, we don't have to give complete power to the doctors and hospital systems; we can go to them and listen to them, use them for what we need and still be responsible for ourselves at the same time.

For example, the Jennifer who doesn't identify herself as a cancer patient, changes her lifestyle, her diet, forgives her parents and takes up exercise and meditation as well as goes into hospital for chemotherapy and radiation treatment is much more likely to heal from cancer than the Jennifer who surrenders to the cancer, does the chemotherapy and radiation and expects the medicine and the doctors to do all the work. There are more and more cases of 'spontaneous remission' from cancer and other serious illnesses happening all the time. You can look them up on the internet and see what they all have in common if you are called to do so.

Labels Come from Trauma

As well as labelling ourselves with a diagnosis, we can label ourselves as a survivor of something traumatic. The problem here is that if we don't grieve properly, give ourselves time to process what happened and move on, we can end up carrying the heavy energy of the trauma around with us for the rest of our life. Talk about having a blocked river!

We do get wounded – yes, we do. But instead of becoming 'expert woundologists', we can choose to heal the wound until it turns into a scar and we can get on with our life. What keeps us stuck in the energy of the trauma is when we keep picking the wound open to check it, or we wear the scar like a badge on our chest, out front, when it's the first thing someone else sees. It's something to talk about, to show someone, something that can grow to be bigger than it actually is.

This may upset you if this is the case with you, but please keep reading. You can continue to put your power into the story of the trauma or you can start to put it into your health and your future. You never have to forget what happened, but it doesn't have to rule you for the rest of your life.

Remember: You are not what happened to you.

'Feeling like yourself again' can be a very difficult process after a trauma because you will never be the same person you were before it happened. Also, you need to grieve the loss of your innocence, to take time to get over the pain that you suffered or whatever it was that you went through. You need to process it in your mind, make sense of it and know that you did the best you could. You need to forgive whoever you need to forgive, including yourself.

It might sound harsh when I say this, but deep down you know that to be well, your soul needs to be free and fast in its vibration, not held back or punished for something that happened a long time ago. You may not be ready to do this yet, and that's okay. Grieving takes time. So you may want to see this material as a seed being planted in you which will grow and blossom when it's ready.

But if you feel it's time, gently allow yourself to be free of past wounding and trauma, to let go of the labels and to be the new you, scars and all. Take the opportunity to become your best, healed, self.

Labels Come from Our Roles

In Chapter 1 I mentioned the chef who said he wouldn't know who he was if he couldn't cook anymore. Roles tend to become labels too. That goes for roles in families as well as professional roles. Everyone knows the eldest child is the most responsible, the middle child is the forgotten one and the youngest one gets spoilt. The new person on the team, the youngest executive on the board, the secretary, the manager, all of these roles have energies that you can tell apart from one another as you read them, right? But they are just roles, they aren't the people inside the roles.

Remember: You are not what you do.

In the movie *Like Water for Chocolate*, the family rule was that the youngest daughter wasn't allowed to marry and had to dedicate her life to looking after her ageing mother. Some families have unwritten rules like this. They have expectations too. And some companies do too. You may be acting out a role or an expectation that you feel has been placed upon you, rather than one you have consciously taken on yourself. But becoming empowered means making conscious choices rather than unconscious ones. You might still need to look after your ageing mother, but do it because you want to rather than because you think you have to.

Transforming Our Labels

'So, what's going to be different for you, Patrick, now that you realize you're no longer depressed?'

'I guess I have no excuse any more for not doing things?'

'Well,' I say, 'if you don't feel well then you have to look after yourself. You can still get sick, or exhausted, or stressed, even if you're not depressed. Bad days and good days happen to everyone.'

Labels like depression give us permission to be sad, to be angry or to stay in bed without feeling guilty about it. But you know what? If you feel that you need a day in bed, you can give yourself permission to have one without needing an excuse for it or feeling guilty about it, label or not. It's called self-care. If an exhausted friend was asking your advice, you'd tell them to stay home and rest, so why not be your own best friend?

This sounds easier than it is, and it takes practice and a high sense of self-worth. But you're working on that, so it will get easier over time. Start by becoming more aware of how you are feeling – the wellness scale can really help here. If you're below 5, then you need to think about doing something for yourself. What do you need to do? Read Chapter 6 for some ideas and look at your emergency self-care list if you have to (*see page 206*). If you're below 2, do you need a day of rest? Do you need to phone a friend? Allow yourself to be yourself, scars and all, without feeling that you have to be performing or doing more than you are able. Once you make friends with yourself this way, you become more relaxed and at ease with yourself – and with life.

Creating Your New Identity

'Do you need to put a label on who you are now?' I ask.

'Well, I guess it would be easier for me to move from one label to another,' says Patrick thoughtfully.

'Okay, then – let's create a better label for you. What would you like it to be?'

'A poet, a lover of life, a person who is great fun, optimistic...' His list goes on and he softens and relaxes as he speaks.

'But these aren't labels,' I say, 'these are qualities, values and skills that you have. Is just being Patrick who encapsulates all of these things enough for you?'

'I guess I always think of Patrick as being depressed,' he says. 'I'd like to think that could change.'

'Repeat after me, "I am Patrick. I deserve to be happy. I give myself permission to live a happy life."'

Patrick repeats the affirmation several times a day every day for several weeks. He visualizes himself as lighter, happier and doing what he loves to do – writing poetry, laughing with friends, going for walks and feeling well. Over time, his image of himself shifts from being a heavy, depressed person who has trouble with life to a lighter, easier-going person who gets into the flow of life. When he comes to see me a month or two later he tells me he's thinking of going back to college to study English literature, something that he loves to talk about but has never felt qualified to do. It is time for him to start investing in who he truly is.

Perhaps you can relate to this story. Do you see yourself as a person who struggles with life? Someone who is always at the wrong end of the stick? Someone who never has any luck, never gets a break, someone who is always suffering? Can you understand how seeing yourself like this actually makes you like this? And how easy it is to slip into that role, especially if the people around you also see you that way and wish to keep you in that space?

You need to spend some time creating a new role for yourself, a new identity. By doing this you are easing your ego into a new space and removing the fear around it. It's as if you've had a starring role in a soap opera for many years, always playing the same part, with the same lines, the same complaints, but now you've been offered a new role, and this time you get a choice.

Here are some questions you can ask yourself to get started:

- 🌿 'Am I seeing the world from a wounded space?'

- 🌿 'How would I like to feel when I wake up in the morning?'

- 🌿 'What would I like to spend more time doing?'

- 🌿 'Who would I be if I wasn't [sick/depressed/etc.]?'

- 🌿 'How would happy me act in [name situation] compared to the me I am now?'

This may seem unsettling at first because we all fear change, but change is inevitable. And you are choosing how you'll change. You're not going into it blindly. Creating a new identity through this work is like sending a scout ahead to see what the landscape in front of you is like. You're testing it out before going there yourself, so it feels safer to you.

Whatever your new identity turns out to be, remember that it's good to feel lighter, healthier and happier. And you'll grow into it!

Connecting with Your Future Healed Self

As you put the work in, you are growing stronger, happier and more confident. The healed you, the well you, the you you long to be, will exist in the future as long as you continue to invest in yourself. Imagine hitting a stable 7–8 as your baseline wellness score. How long will it take you to get to this level of wellness? One year? Three years? Five years? Think about it.

But I do need to be clear that *your future healed self is not your ideal self.* Your ideal self is an idea of who you think you should be and is most likely based on something that isn't achievable for a human being. It's always perfect, never messes up, never gets sick and always does an impeccable job. Sounds familiar? Well, I'm sorry to break this to you, but *your ideal self will never exist.*

Your future healed self *will* make mistakes, but they won't blame themselves for them, they'll learn from them and move on from them as fast as they are able. Your future healed self may lose their temper, get angry and shout, but they'll get over it faster than you do now. Your future healed self may still have their heart broken, trust the wrong person or end up in a situation that's not healthy. But they will see it more quickly, realize what they need to do and remedy the situation instead of putting up with it or holding on to grudges or emotional pain.

So stop making your future healed self into an impossible dream, into something that lives on a pedestal and is unobtainable. That's an ideal, and that doesn't exist. The more human you give yourself permission to be, the less scary being your future healed self becomes. And the less scary it becomes, the more likely it'll be that you'll make the commitment to get to that space for yourself.

EXERCISE

Connecting with Your Future Healed Self

See, feel and know that in the future there is a healed version of you – if you are determined and committed to the work then that person exists, right?

❖ Close your eyes, come into your body and imagine that you are moving forwards in time to find your healed self. Imagine a time when you are happy, healthy and scoring highly on your wellness scale, a time when you regularly wake up and feel good. Check in with yourself to get an idea of how far into the future this is. Is it one year away? Two years? Six months?

❖ Invite your wise healed self to come and visit you now for a chat. You can do this anytime you feel you need extra support. How do you do it? Simply soften your body, soften your heart and open up to a visit from your healed self. Imagine they're in the room with you now. If this isn't working, then you can imagine going to a safe space in nature, perhaps one you've been to already, and finding your healed self there waiting for you. Or you can go to a space in nature and wait for them to come to you. Do whatever feels the most natural for you.

❖ Tell them what's going on for you and where you feel you need the most help. Ask if they have any advice for you and if there's anything you need to know. Listen with your heart, not your head. Take your time and be slow and open to hearing something you might not want to hear. Take heed of the advice and make a commitment to yourself to carry it out if you are ready to do so.

❖ When you've finished chatting, if it feels right to shake hands or hug your healed self, then do so. Thank them, allow the images to dissolve away and come back fully to the room.

❖ You may want to write down whatever came up for you in your notebook. It will be interesting to read back over your wellness journey as you move closer to becoming your healed self.

❖ Before you close your notebook, read what you were told you needed to do now. Can you do it? Will you do it? What's in the way? Make a note of that too.

Don't worry if you didn't meet your healed self during this exercise – maybe you didn't see them, but did you feel them? Did you get a sense of them there, waiting patiently, proud of all the work you're doing? They are. Maybe you're just not ready to hear what they have to say at the moment. Trust that all is well and come back later and try this again.

Your Healing Affects Your Family

Do you like who you are becoming? Are you noticing that your stress levels are going down, that you are waking up with more enthusiasm for your day? On your wellness scale, are you mostly over 5 now? Would you like to shift that up to 6 or 7?

If Aunty Mary doesn't like it, will you stop changing? Is it your problem that she's not happy that you're beginning to express yourself more at the dinner table? Or dancing in public? Or singing? Or is it her problem? Is she resentful because she never afforded herself the time or space to do that? Why do you get to do it and not her?

I'm not being funny here: when people identify themselves as the role they play in the family, they feed energy into all the other roles too, based on the other people's usual behaviour. And if you were the quiet one, the dependable one, the one who always picked up the pieces and cleaned up the mess, and you're not that any more, well, you've thrown out the whole family system, haven't you? Everyone has to stop and take stock of how your new self impacts on them.

So, if an argument breaks out between you and someone you love, know that it will pass, it's just the energies recalibrating, the old ties being cut, the constellations being reshaped. You might want to do the tie-cutting exercises until the dust settles, so to speak. And here's an exercise you can use to clear the air between you and someone who is upset.

EXERCISE

Heal the Space Between You and Someone You're Fighting With

Do this yourself, by yourself, alone, just you. You don't need to report anything back to anyone, you don't need to phone anyone and tell them what you're doing or what you've done. Just notice if there's an energy shift between you and the person after you've done the work.

❖ Feel everything you're feeling. It's okay. Be angry, be upset, it's how you are. Breathe it out and bring yourself into your heart centre.

✦ Visualize the person in question and notice how far away they feel from you. Ask yourself what is in the gap between you and them.

✦ Imagine that you step out of your body and go up to a higher level of wisdom, compassion and love. See them doing the same thing. You're accessing a higher aspect of yourself, an aspect you can call your 'higher self'.

✦ Imagine your higher self and the other person's higher self meeting for a chat. It could be in a landscape, at your favourite café, at a familiar place, all in your mind's eye. Talk it out, see if there is something you're missing, some fundamental problem that you can solve together at this higher level. Apologize for things being the way they are, for the misunderstanding and miscommunication. Listen to what the other person's higher self says to you. (Step out of the way for this. Don't use your brain and ego to fill in the gaps, just be silent for a while and something will come in.) Know that the other person's higher self can take a higher perspective of the situation and is not angry at you. Although their adult, physical aspect may still be angry, their higher self knows what you're going through and just wants validation for what they're going through too.

✦ Imagine there's a softness between your higher self and the other person's higher self. If you can, fill the space with love. If you can't, come back and try again later.

✦ When you feel the conversation has ended, gently dissolve away all the images and come back into your body. Imagine the other person is going back into their body too, wherever they are. Feel that the new information your higher selves have shared is lifting a weight from both of you. Feel that your faces soften and your hearts open a little bit to each other. Breathe out any animosity and anger that you're still holding on to in your body. How does it feel now between you?

The purpose of this exercise is not to enable you to have your own way, nor to enable the other person to breach your boundaries in an unhealthy way, it's just to clear the air between you. So don't use it to attack the other person. Your higher self really doesn't work that way. If you find you're doing that, then stop – it's your ego getting in the way. Take some time out and make sure your ego feels validated and listened to, and then check in with yourself to heal any other aspect of yourself that needs healing before you try again.

In my experience, most arguments are due to poor communication, so clearing the air and creating space enables you to focus on what the issue is, gain clarity and perhaps find a solution that could work for both parties. Just creating space to talk takes the emotional charge out of the air between you and the other person and they are more likely to be reasonable when you approach them face to face to sort things out.

Know that if there's been a big shift in you, you may have to search to find common ground. Understand that if the other person isn't willing to heal or change their frame of reference, there may be no common ground to find. But you're not going to compromise your wellness for someone else's identity issue, are you? You're too busy creating a life you love.

Create a Life You Love

So here we are, coming to the end of this book. What is left for you to do? Create a life you love. You deserve it, and why not? You've put the work in.

I'm going to take a brief look here at how to create your best life. We've done so much work releasing old things that now it's time to create some things of a higher vibration to fill the space. But creating a life you love takes a lot more information than I can put in the final half of the final chapter of a book and you might want to consider investing some more time in researching this. Check out the resources list at the back of this book and see where it takes you.

Follow Your Joy

When you're used to surviving most of the time, learning how to live from a space of joy can feel like a foreign country. Joy has a high vibration and it can feel uncomfortable at first if you don't truly resonate with it. As you get through the work in this book you'll notice, however, that feeling lighter and happier becomes easier. You may even find yourself deliberately looking for things to keep that feeling of happiness for longer, and this is a positive signal that healing has happened.

Reasons why you're afraid to truly feel joyful could include that you've never felt that way before, or perhaps you did once and then something bad happened. Don't let that stop you – you're a different person now and you're able to handle it. You're allowed to be happy without feeling guilty about it. You're allowed to be happy even if people in your family are suffering. You're allowed to feel light and radiant when others are feeling heavy and ill. Don't apologize for your newfound vibrancy; instead, see yourself as a positive role model. If you can do it, maybe you'll inspire others to do it too.

Being joyful doesn't mean you're not compassionate or that you're 'full of yourself'. Yes, others may not understand you or may even be jealous of you. This is what happens when they see someone they identify themselves with shifting into a different space. All the work you've done in this chapter on your identity affects other people too. People become very attached to how they see the world, and they don't like to change that. But remember, as long as you're not being selfish and taking more than you need, you'll have more space for other people then before and you'll have more energy available. And you can choose where you spend it.

In my book *Energy Healing*, I teach you how to pull down a high-vibrational healing energy which you can use to heal yourself. In that book I also look at how being healed affects the people around you and give you exercises to help you gently heal your family system. I highly recommend that book as a complement to the work you're doing here.

In the meantime, here's an exercise you can try to move one step closer to joy on the vibrational energy scale.

EXERCISE

Allow More Joy into Your Life

❖ Sit in a quiet space where you won't be disturbed. Feel your feet on the ground, connect to the Earth. Breathe out any heaviness, any fear, any anxiety.

❖ Say out loud: 'It is safe to be happy.'

❖ Breathe out anything in yourself that doesn't feel safe.

❖ Say out loud: 'I give myself permission to feel more joy in my life.'

❖ Wait. See how that sits with you. Does it resonate? Is there more work to do? If you're anxious, breathe out the anxiety and say it again when you feel more settled.

❖ Imagine that joy is right there waiting for you. All you have to do is let it in. What does that feel like? What does joy feel like? Is it overwhelming?

❖ Breathe and allow joy to come closer in to you, just a little bit. Can you feel a shift in your energy? Again, connect to the ground if you need to.

❖ If joy is a great big ball of dancing light and it's coming closer to you right now, what do you have to let go of to embrace it? Take this slowly. Breathe deeply. This is a state of mind, a lifestyle change, not something fleeting.

❖ Imagine the ball of light is toning down its frequency and vibration so that it's softer and more comfortable for you. Imagine that at the same time you're also raising your vibration so you match the joy that little bit more.

❖ Your energies shift and move up to the light and the light comes down to you.

❖ Breathe.

❖ Let the ball of light, of peace, calm, happiness, whatever you want to call it now, come into your body, so that you're surrounded by a big ball of light.

❖ Breathe it in, and breathe in anything in yourself that's struggling, that's resisting. You might want to reassure these aspects of yourself that they're safe and it's okay to be happy. You might want to do the 'Healing an Aspect of Yourself' exercise (*see page 152*) at this point if they need more time with you, if they want to be heard.

❖ As you tune yourself into joy, you feel stronger, brighter, healthier.

❖ Stay with this for as long as you can, then let go of the breath, of the images, and let the light soften in your mind's eye as you bring your awareness back into the room you're in.

❖ Write in your journal anything that you feel you need to remember to work on later. You're doing great.

The more you do this, the safer you feel, and the more natural it becomes to feel joy. Some days it feels different from others, depending on what's going on for you. It can be just as intense to feel joy as to feel emotional pain. Our body does the best that it can when it's processing emotions, and they can feel overwhelming at times. But as long as you remember that you can connect to the Earth and ground yourself and slow everything down, you'll be able to manage it all.

❋❋❋❋

Manifesting with the Law of Attraction

> *'If there is something that you desire and it is not
> coming to you, it always means the same thing. You
> are not a vibrational match to your own desire.'*
>
> ABRAHAM-HICKS

Here I'm going to give you a brief introduction to how to use the Law of Attraction to manifest the life you want. I'm making it simple, but in fact it's complex and simple at the same time!

The Law of Attraction pretty much says, 'Like attracts like.' So if you think heavy thoughts all the time, you create heavy emotions, which then go into a cycle to create more heavy thoughts. So, overall, you are heavy, and you attract heavy things in to your energy field. It gets difficult to break out of this – it's a bit like sliding down the wellness scale to 2. Sadness, slowness, negativity, fear, anger, even hatred can become attracted to you if you're at level 2, because that's the vibration that you are resonating with. There's no point trying to manifest anything great when you're there; just try to get well.

It takes a lot of energy to break out of level 2 because the energies are so heavy, that's why we created the emergency self-care list (*see page 206*). With the help of this, and the other exercises, you will be able to break out of a 2 and move up the scale to 3, 4 and 5. When your baseline wellness scale is over 5, you resonate with higher-vibrational thoughts, nice things happen to you and you start to look for more nice things, which then happen to you. When you shift from 2 to 5, there's a big difference in what you are noticing and what is around you. There is more peace and calm, more space to breathe. You might even start to become aware of what it is you do love and start to allow yourself to have more of that.

If you're feeling the vibration of 5, you're acting out of 5 and you're receiving things that are at 5. Make sense? But you can still wake up at 5 on your wellness scale and decide you're going to have a crappy day because you're not looking forward to something that's planned. You then look for all the crappy things in the day and I promise you will find them. I said to a client once, 'If you look for the dog poo, you will find the dog poo.' There is always plenty of it if you go looking... So don't look for it. And if something does happen to upset you, think of it as a blip on the radar, process it and let it go, so you can move up and on to better things.

When your baseline scale is 7, 8 or 9 (well done!), you're on the path to joy. You're in the flow, things come easily to you and you resonate with laughter, happiness, ease and gratitude. You don't consider looking for dog poo because you have no interest in it. You're filling yourself up with beauty and peace, people you love, things you enjoy. This is your natural way of being – babies are born like this. You attract in high-vibrational energies, so you can start to deliberately create the amazing things that you want for your life. It's time to allow ourselves to embrace our natural, happy selves. The more of us who feel safe to do this, the better the world becomes for us all.

So, keep up your great work on your wellness scale. That's a fundamental part of manifesting a life that you love.

Co-Creation Means Creating with the Universe

Whether you believe in God or not, you have to agree that some sort of universe exists, and it's bigger than your ego. We don't need to go deeply into spiritual beliefs here, only to say that even if you consider yourself the centre of your universe, which you are, then you are the beneficent creator of your own life and it's time to work more favourably with yourself.

So you can either come from the stance that your higher self is the creator of the universe or you can believe that the universe is God or Source energy, the creator of all things. It honestly doesn't matter. If you want to embrace working with the Law of Attraction, both of these ideas are valid. For sake of argument, let's say that the universe is the greater, wiser part of you that connects to all other living things, and it's only by working *with* this aspect of yourself, *in alignment with all the other aspects*, that you can create a life that you truly love. Phew!

Things you need to know before you start:

* Co-creation means you and the universe create your life together. But you have to make the first move. Once you know what it is that you want to create, you must take inspired action towards your goals. Inspired action means that you receive ideas from inspiration and then take action on them. Your inspiration comes from your gut instinct – your intuition – not just from your brain. Once the universe 'sees' you taking steps towards something that you want, it will take similar steps towards it on your behalf.

※ If you become desperate, needy and attached to what you want, you push it away. Desperation and neediness are low-level vibrations that act like a magnet repelling your heart's desire. And being too attached to something creates very tight energy ties between you and whatever it is. These are unhealthy for you, so let them all go and be open to what may happen.

※ The universe only 'gives' you something if it is for the highest good of all. So even if you really, really want it and move to co-creating it, it still may not be for the highest good. You will never have all the answers; instead you need to have faith and trust. So, let go of attachment and, again, be open to what might happen in its place.

※ The universe works best when the energies are fast and light. So having fun, being happy and joyful and always bringing gratitude into your life yield quicker results than being as serious as if you're playing a game of chess with everything at stake.

Working with the Law of Attraction can be as complex as a game of chess, but nobody's watching, it's just you and the universe, so try out a few moves and see what works and what doesn't. It's much more fun to focus on learning this game than to be back in victim modality, attracting in drama and carrying heaps of emotional pain. Just know that if you get to this stage in your life and you're ready for it, it's like playing a big game where everybody wins.

So What Is It Exactly That You Want to Create?

Remember to get the three essentials right first: *where* you are, *what* you do and *who* you're with.

Some of you may want a new house, or to go visiting new places or exploring new countries. Some of you may want to change job or career, get a new education or even a vocation. And some of you are looking for love, a new relationship or a family.

If you believe that changing these things will be difficult, then it will be difficult. It's not just about what your mind believes, it's also about your inner self, all the aspects of yourself, your limiting beliefs and your feelings of self-worth, self-esteem and self-confidence. Mostly it's about whether you deeply, truly believe that you deserve whatever it is that you want.

Make a list of all the things you'd like to have in your life. Some of them will be simpler than others. Whatever they are, by writing them down and working through your limiting beliefs (why you feel you can't have them), you start to shift the energies around them. Then you can take it to the next stage.

Do You Believe You Can Have It?

It's possible that you have a core belief that you'll never have enough money, based on your parents acting as if they never had enough money. It's also possible you believe that you'll never be good enough to sell a painting in an auction, to have a fashion show with your designs or to compose music that tops the charts. But does your soul long to create these things?

If it lights you up, it's your talent. If you can clear the limiting belief that you're not allowed to shine your light at its brightest, then you can step into that talent. Once you're there, you need to trust that you will get all that you need to allow you take it to the next level, whatever that may be. Sounds simple and yet it's complex, isn't it? That's why so many people 'fail' at manifesting: because they don't clear their complex issues around why they can't have what they want.

Be Real

Just because you decide you want to become a therapist, that doesn't mean that people will suddenly start knocking on your door looking for healing. You have to do all the practical things, too, like investing in the training, taking the classes, purchasing insurance and tell people you're available. This is the co-creation part: you spend time getting clear about what type of therapy you want to do, then sign up for the class. You can't give up a source of income for a dream, particularly if you have no other source of income. So, keep it real and keep your day job, but also keep moving in the direction of what you want.

It's never too late to train in something new; we live in a world where you can take up a new skill at any age of your life. If you open your mind to possibilities, more possibilities come to you. And it's never too late for more love to come into your life, whether that means clearing issues in an old relationship and taking it to a new level, opening your door to someone completely new, loving yourself more or adopting a rescue dog.

'Fake It till You Make It' Doesn't Work

Many spiritual teachers who specialize in Law of Attraction say, 'Now that you know what you want, imagine that you already have it, with emotion, and it will come to you.' I don't believe this works, because part of us knows that we don't already have it. This aspect of us may still think we don't deserve it, and worse than that, there could be an aspect of us that wants to sabotage the whole thing just to prove it's correct.

To get around this, you need to work with your internal saboteur, the angry part of you that wants to wreck everything you've created. It can take time, years even, before you come to an arrangement whereby they transform into a helpful ally. Bringing your awareness to this part of yourself is hard work and you might need to get support. Working through the exercises in Chapter 3 again will help. A daily spiritual practice will make sure that all the aspects of you are looked after and that you have no parts that are aching and ready to damage you because they're angry you're not paying them attention. High self-worth and self-esteem really help a lot too.

Raise the Vibration for Manifestation

Being grateful for everything dissolves away pain, hurt, fear and anxiety and brings us up and out of wherever we are into something better. When we're at level 2 on the wellness scale, simply being grateful for the awareness that we're at level 2 changes the energy for the better.

This next energy technique will also help shift the vibrations that are blocking your manifestations. Even if you don't truly believe you'll get everything you want, this technique will enable you to recognize your limiting beliefs, so you can do further work on them. You can also use it to soften and heal your limiting beliefs so you can start embracing what you could be creating and let go of what you believe is stopping you.

EXERCISE

Energy Technique for Manifestation

To get the most out of this exercise, be in a quiet place, centred and grounded, with a notebook and pen.

❖ Start by clearing your energy and cutting ties from relationships, projects or anything that you've invested too much of yourself into. You need all of the resources that are available to you to do this work, so if someone pops into your head that you've given your energy to, say thank you to them and ask them to release your energy back to you. Check to see if you have their energy too and release that back to them, just as before.

❖ When you're feeling in balance and ready, write down a list of everything you're asking the universe for. Write it like a letter if you want to ('Dear Universe, please can you give me a trip to Hawaii?') and keep writing till you've finished.

❖ Go back and read the list, feeling into each thing you're asking for and asking yourself if you believe you can have it 100 per cent. Write down the percentage you believe it. (For example, you could believe 50 per cent that a holiday to Hawaii for the whole family will come to you, but believe 100 per cent that you'll get an upgrade for your computer.) It's about gaining awareness of your blocks.

❖ Take a new page and write down all the limiting beliefs that are stopping you from believing you will receive an item from your list. Is that all? Is there an underlying limiting belief you need to clear? If you're not sure, just ask yourself or write down 'and any other limiting belief that I'm not aware of'.

❖ Now it's healing time. Close the notebook and hold it in your hand, go into your heart and tune in to the energy of gratitude, as if you're a radio tuning into a radio station. Breathe in gratitude and breathe out anything that is not gratitude until you feel lighter, more balanced, grounded. Spend some time feeling grateful for the opportunity to do this work right now.

❖ Say the following:

> *'Thank you for this chance to have my best life.*
>
> *I give myself permission to let go of whatever is in the way of having my best life now.*
>
> *Thank you. I am ready and open to receive healing love, light and joy.*
>
> *Thank you, thank you, thank you, thank you.'*

❖ Breathe in gratitude again and breathe out anything that is not gratitude. Do this for several breaths. The more you do it, the longer you can hold on to the energy.

❖ Then let it dissolve and return to what you were doing.

✳✳✳✳

This isn't a magic trick, a spell or a quick fix. You might need to do this many, many times before you feel any real shift. And you might, by doing this, shake up something in yourself that is holding you back but is big scary stuff. Giving yourself permission to let go of what is in the way could have an impact in your physical world too. You can't hide from it if you want to move forwards. So, work with it, surrender to it. You know how to now.

It's so much better to focus on creating your best life than to go looking for the dog poo. Because you know you'll find dog poo and it's a lot more exciting to find the things you actually want, and celebrate as they begin to show up in your life.

Conclusion

I f you've picked up this book and read it quickly from cover to cover, you may not have made many changes in your life yet, but know that seeds have been planted and there is time for you to nurture them and grow.

If you've gone through it slowly, spending time with all the exercises, you'll be seeing some changes already. Keep going.

And if this is your second or third reading, you can move on to dip in and out of the book whenever you feel that you need some extra support. See if it opens to a page that you need to read at a particular moment in time. Absorb some of the case studies and feel that there is hope, that you can change the things that you feel aren't working in your life. And if you still feel overwhelmed by what you think you need to do, please do get some help and don't be afraid to ask for it. See a psychotherapist for your mind or a shamanic healer for your soul. Perhaps you need a life coach to help you get the balance right or an NLP practitioner for thought patterns that just won't shift. See a nutritionist if you need help changing your diet, go to your doctor if you are in pain. See whichever specialist can help you with whatever it is that ails you. But don't sit with it. It won't go away – in fact it will just get worse. So sort it out.

The world needs happy, healthy, passionate, motivated, bright, beautiful people in it. The world needs people who care for other people without compromising themselves while doing it. People who look after themselves have more energy to give and they give in a clear, healthy way with no strings attached.

I want to live in a world where people love one another for who they are, not for what they do for one another. Where people respect one another, even if they don't fully understand or agree with one another. Where people give one another space to be happy, to be themselves, and don't need to control one another. Where people are responsible for their own emotional health and happiness and create healthy, loving communities when they come together and support one another.

That world starts right here, right now, with you. I lift my green juice and toast to your wellness today and for many years to come.

Choosing the Right Therapist and Therapy

Asking for Help

This section is by no means complete, but throughout the book I've said, 'Don't be afraid to ask for help,' so I want to give you some understanding of what type of help there is. In my years of experience as a therapist, I've found that clients feel disempowered at times by therapists. My aim here is to give you information that will empower you to ask good questions before you make a booking and to know your rights when it comes to therapy, so that you can make the right decision for yourself based on your own good judgement and intuition.

Many people decide to train in a specific therapy and become a therapist instead of actually going into process as a client and doing the work they need to do. If you do want to become a therapist, you'll become a stronger, more authentic therapist if you begin as a client and make a good start on your own work before beginning any training programmes. You'll also gain the knowledge of what it's like to be a client, which will enhance your personal skills if you decide to become a therapist!

A Short Note on Regulating Bodies

A regulating body is a group or organization that creates rules, standards and guidelines for correct practice. It is the place to go to find a credible professional therapist in a specific field of work. This may sound technical, but if something goes wrong during a session, it's good to have this information from the outset.

There are two of types of regulating body: statutory regulating bodies (run by the state or government) and non-statutory or self-regulating bodies (independent bodies that run themselves). It is usually a long and difficult process to be listed as an accredited practitioner for a state-regulated body; self-regulating bodies are much less rigorous, but the standards may not be as high, depending on who is running the body in question. You won't find a state-regulating body for most complementary therapies, as the state doesn't tend to get involved in holistic work; however, it does take an active interest in psychology and psychotherapy, which is why I'm mentioning this here. In the USA, licences will usually be required for any practising psychotherapist; however, it is quite different in Europe and the rest of the world.

The advantage of looking up a regulating body for a therapist is that you have a comeback as a client if something goes wrong. You also have the expectation of a certain standard of practice from your therapist. If the rules for correct practice are not adhered to by the practitioner, you have a right to make a complaint to the regulating body and the consequences for the therapist may include investigation leading to being struck off the register of practitioners.

If you want to find a register of practitioners for a particular therapy before choosing your therapist, you can do a web search. Types of keywords you could use could be 'regulating body for reflexology in Ireland'. Please note that looking up something like 'register of practitioners for Reiki in London' could actually bring up a website where practitioners pay to be listed and aren't covered by any regulation whatsoever.

Do visit the websites you get in your search results and make up your own mind based on the information you find there. You can also look up a register of practitioners related to a specific school or college to find past pupils, which could be a good idea if a school you know of has a good reputation. Then you can contact the therapists and ask them the questions I give you here (*below*).

At the end of the day, a good therapy session still comes down to your confidence in your therapist and the relationship between you, so the next section will give you some guidelines and give you questions to ask any therapist in advance of booking a session.

Choosing a Psychotherapist

There are so many types of therapy to choose from it can be very confusing. I've listed and categorized some of the therapies here to make it a bit easier. I haven't included all the different types that exist, just the commoner ones. My descriptions aren't definitive; they are brief, to give you a taste of what each therapy is about. If something appeals to you, I do urge you to look further into it to make up your mind.

Counselling: Talking with someone to gain perspective on your life situation. This is non-directive – no advice is given and it is driven by the client, i.e. the client chooses what to talk about. It usually takes about four to six sessions of counselling to work through an issue.

Psychotherapy: This can be more directive in that once it's clear what the client is looking to do, the therapist takes a more active role. They can suggest techniques and a direction to work in, using different processes to help create transformation. There may be homework in the form of tasks to do (such as keeping a journal), so for this reason several sessions may be required.

Psychotherapy is really more about the relationship you create with the therapist than the type of therapy they are offering. So you do need to make an emotional connection with your therapist. Many psychotherapists use an integrative approach, which means that they are versed in several different modes of therapy and they blend them together as needed in a session. The number of sessions that are required for psychotherapy/counselling are set between you and the therapist and can be decided upfront or on a session-by-session basis. You do have rights to negotiate this, so if a psychotherapist demands six sessions' payment upfront and you ask for a trial session or to pay on a session-by-session basis and they don't waver, it's a signal to you as to how the sessions themselves may proceed. Remember, if you feel you aren't enjoying the process, aren't connecting with the therapist or aren't comfortable with them, you can end the sessions at any time.

Psychoanalysis: A very intensive therapy, where the psychoanalyst studies your thought patterns and history and makes a diagnosis over many sessions. You do most of the talking, the therapist asks questions and traditionally sits behind you, out of eye contact. This may involve going back to trauma and childhood events, talking about dreams, etc.

Bereavement Counselling: A specialized form of counselling that helps you move on from a loss in your life – any kind of loss, not just the loss of a loved one.

Cognitive Behavioural Therapy: This psychotherapeutic process concentrates on looking at your thought patterns and teaching you ways to change them to healthier ones.

Gestalt: A process which uses talking and feeling to work through problems. This type of therapy offers a holistic approach, working with the emotional body. It can be very powerful and at times it may feel like the mindfulness energy-healing exercises in this book.

Human Givens: A type of psychotherapy that works on a framework based on the idea that people have a set of needs that have to be met.

Transpersonal Therapy: Psychotherapy that works with a belief in God or something greater than us to help manage life situations.

Other forms of therapy may include art therapy, brief therapy, family therapy, group therapy, play therapy, positive psychology and transactional therapy. You can see there are many different forms!

It's very useful to talk about the therapy process with the therapist, i.e. check in and tell them you're really benefitting from the sessions, or let them know if you're not happy. Talking about the therapy process with the therapist can dramatically improve the results, as both of you are more aware of what is going on. Sometimes it can be your resistance to the work making you unhappy with the therapy rather than anything the therapist is doing.

Group therapy is when a group of people go into process together, though not always at the same time. If you take part in it, you will be exposed to other people's processes. If you're not ready for it and you pick up on their energies as well as the ones you're already trying to work with, it can really make things difficult for you. Keep in mind that a one-to-one session may be what you need if you're feeling fragile.

Questions to Ask a Psychotherapist/Counsellor

❋   'How long have you been in practice?'

❋   'Are you a member of an accrediting body?/Do you have a licence?'

❋   'Where did you get your degree?'

❋   'How much do you charge for your sessions?'

❋   'Do I need to sign up for a certain number of sessions?'

⚘ 'Do you have a cancellation policy?'

⚘ 'Do you accept personal health insurance?'

Choosing the Right Energy Therapy

When thinking about the number of energy therapies now available, it can be overwhelming to work out what you need. Please know that, like psychotherapy, the success of energy healing is more about the relationship between you and the therapist than about the therapy itself. There may be some very gifted energy healers out there who aren't qualified or certified in mainstream modalities (ways of working) and you could be missing out if you decide not to see them for that reason.

Every therapist will be different, and every session will be different, but there are some commonalities, such as when receiving energy healing there is no need for you to remove your clothing. You will typically lie down and the therapist will place their hands on or over your body, drawing down the universal life-force energy into your biofield. These therapies can work over plaster casts if you have a broken limb; they can also work over distance if you can't make it into the therapist's office for a treatment.

Types of energy therapies include (but are not exclusive to):

⚘ bioenergy healing

⚘ crystal healing

⚘ EmoTrance

⚘ Hands of Light holistic healing

- Integrated Energy Therapy (IET)

- Johrei

- Life Alignment therapy

- past-life regression

- pranic healing

- Quantum Touch

- Rahanni Celestial Healing

- Reconnection healing

- Reiki (there are many forms – Usui, Karuna, Tibetan, Angelic, Tera Mai, Rainbow, Dragon, Kundalini – all of which have different methods to access the universal life-force energy)

- Restorative Touch

- Sakura

- Seichem

- ThetaHealing®

You can research each type of healing if you wish to know more about it. I would also suggest that you look for a recommendation from someone who has been to the healer you are considering. Remember, this is more about the healer than about the modality of healing; some people are born to be healers and may not even have trained formally, so they may simply offer you 'spiritual healing'. Others who have trained for years may not be natural healers, but may do a great job helping you release energies and acting as a witness for you. You will only know if you try it.

Many therapists tend to mix several therapies together and don't usually tell the client in advance, so ask when booking if it's pure Reiki, for example, or if they combine it with something else.

Remember everyone is different, and the training is different too. Each Reiki Master, for example, will teach in their own way, so Reiki students will all receive different training. When looking for a therapist, do your homework first: look at their website, read their blog, get a feel for their energy. Nowadays, there is online training available for energy healers and you can complete a master's programme over a very short period of time. This doesn't make you a master therapist. However, some people call themselves that regardless. You need to be sure that you are going to a well-practised professional. It's useful to ask some, or all, of the following questions.

Questions to Ask an Energy Therapist

- ✻ 'How long have you been providing energy-healing treatments?'

- ✻ 'How much do you charge for a session?'

- ✻ 'What level of training do you have?'

- ✻ 'Where did you train?/Was your training in person with a teacher in a hands-on setting or online?'

- ✻ 'When did you complete your training?'

- ✻ 'How many client hours have you completed?'

- ⚘ 'Have you got full public liability insurance?'

- ⚘ 'Can I contact one of your clients for a reference?'

- ⚘ 'What should I expect in a session?'

- ⚘ 'Do you practise healing on yourself every day?'

If the therapist gets worried or angry with you for asking these questions, they might not be the right person for you. The last question, about self-healing and self-care, is very important – as a therapist, they will be seeing many people, and if they don't look after themselves, clear and raise their own vibrations, they may be passing their clients' energy over to you, and you don't want that.

Psychic readings are *not* part of an energy-healing session. After the session, if the therapist has information for you based on what they have read in your energies, treat it as information that is true for that therapist at that moment.

Nothing has to be set in stone. Everything can change. Sometimes additional information from a therapist is useful, such as 'You're not really grounded in your body. Perhaps you could spend some time focusing on that and then you'll feel better.' Don't deeply embrace everything you hear, though. Only pay attention to it if it resonates with you. As you do your work, you'll get clearer on what your work is, and you'll be more empowered to decide yourself what you need to do.

Therapies That Combine Talking and Energy Healing

The following therapies combine talking with energetic healing (and again, there are probably many more therapies in existence than listed here):

Emotional Freedom Technique (EFT): Uses tapping on energy points and affirmations in a set framework to shift energy and work with thought patterns.

Energy Coaching: There are many coaches out there offering energy work; be clear, however, that coaching isn't always therapeutic. (Imagine a coach on a running field shouting at an athlete!) Coaching can help you set goals and become more confident, while therapy is something that I believe should be loving, gentle and transformational.

Hypnotherapy: The therapist goes into your subconscious mind and inserts a script or a program to change behaviour or transform an irrational fear. It can involve energy work or not, depending on the therapist.

Shamanism: Shamanic methods vary dramatically, depending on the training and background of the practitioner. You really need to investigate the therapist before you book a shamanic healing session. Do find out where they trained and how long they have been in practice. Consider getting a recommendation before booking, as this therapy really does depend on the individual practitioner.

Therapies That Work with the Body

Even though they are focused directly on the physical body, bodywork therapies can really help release blocked emotions and are a great complement to any energy work or psychotherapeutic work you may be doing.

Massage: There are many different types of massage, depending on how deep and strong a treatment you wish to receive. You have a right to know if the massage therapist incorporates energy healing with the massage: sometimes practitioners 'close the session' with Reiki because it's nice, but that might not be what you expected. You can tell them to stop if you're unhappy with it.

Reflexology: Using pressure points on the feet to heal the whole body energetically.

Reiki Massage: The therapist combines Reiki with physical massage.

Rolfing: Releasing energies within the connecting fibres and tissues in the body.

Shiatsu: A type of massage where the therapist can release trapped energies from the muscles as well as work with the physical muscles in the body.

The questions to ask before booking a bodywork treatment are similar to the ones already listed above.

Combining Bodywork with Energy Healing

You can incorporate energy healing into body movements to create a strong, grounding practice that will keep you healthy. Healing may not always be the intention behind a bodywork class, but sometimes you'll find it 'sneaks' its way in regardless. Make sure the facilitator is experienced and you feel safe within the group. Try a drop-in class before you sign up for a whole term. This type of practice is more about maintenance of a good energetic state than a portal into deep transformational work. However, people have been known to experience deep healing during this type of work, even though it's not necessarily the intention behind the class.

* Biodanza

* Chakra dancing

* Qigong

* Seven Rhythms dancing

* Tai chi

* Yoga. There are many traditional forms of Yoga such as Astanga, Hatha, Kundalini, Raja, etc., and many new non-traditional forms such as Anti-Gravity, Bikram, Iyengar and Laughter, to name a few.

Therapies for the Environment

You might find after doing energy work that you want to change the energies in your house or in your place of work.

Feng Shui: The practitioner will come and survey your building and give recommendations on where to put particular types of furniture, what colours to use and how to position items for the optimum energy flow.

House/Land Clearing: There are land healers who are shamans. They can come to your house/workplace and work directly with energy blocks in the land. If the energy is being disrupted by a power line, they can help you work around it to improve the general energy flow in the space.

* * * *

How I Can Help You

My mission is 'to heal the world by teaching people how to heal themselves' and to that end my website has many resources, some of them free, to help further your energy-healing journey. Visit www.abby-wynne.com for more information, sign up for my email list and receive weekly energy-healing tips in your inbox along with a free guided meditation.

My Other Books

Energy Healing for Everyone: A Practical Guide to Self-Healing (Balboa Press, 2012). Exercises and practical ideas to help you bring energy healing into your life.

Spiritual Tips for Enlightenment: Practical Spirituality for Every Week of the Year (CreateSpace Independent Publishing Platform, 2013). Practical ways to bring spirituality into your life.

Energy Healing: Unlock Your Potential as a Healer and Bring Healing into Your Everyday Life (Hay House, 2015). Part of Hay House Basics series. A complete course to bring you to a confident place where you know you can heal yourself.

Downloadable Audio Files

I have recorded several healing meditations and healing sessions to support you as you work. Some of them are similar to the exercises in this book and they may enable you to work through blocks and reach a deeper level. Let my voice guide you through a healing session instead of popping in and out of the text in the book and breaking your awareness in the process. This way you can relax into your work at a deeper level.

I also have free meditations on SoundCloud, which you can download as an app and have on your mobile device.

Classes and Sessions

I offer online classes, such as my 21-day 'Raise Your Vibration Bootcamp' to help you develop your own spiritual practice (www.RaiseYourVibrationBootcamp.com) and a healing circle, which you can join and then receive energy healing from me twice a month. Visit www.abby-wynne.com for more information.

I often have a waiting list for one-to-one Skype healing sessions; however, my intention is to continue seeing clients. If you have an issue that you cannot work through yourself and want my direct help, contact me and we can plan something together.

Further Reading

You can heal yourself and then harness the power of the energy around you to create the life you've always wanted. Don't take my word for it, go read what these other people say and try it for yourself! Here are some of the books that have helped me on my own healing journey. These are some of my favourites, but there are lots more out there too, so choose something that resonates with you and see where it will bring you.

Albert Ellis, *How to Stubbornly Refuse to Make Yourself Miserable About Anything – Yes, Anything!* (Citadel Press, 1988). A key book in Rational Emotive Behaviour Therapy, helping you work with mental patterns to reshape them into something healthier for you.

Elizabeth Gilbert, *Big Magic* (Bloomsbury, 2015). A wonderful book about creativity, ideas, authenticity and creative living.

Louise Hay, *You Can Heal Your Life* (Hay House, 2004). Reviews the different parts of the body and what it means when there is illness, dis-ease or blocks in them.

Sandra Ingerman, *Soul Retrieval* (Harper One, 2010). A remarkable book about our life-force energy and the shamanic technique of soul retrieval.

Byron Katie, *Loving What Is: Four Questions That Can Change Your Life* (Rider, 2002). Transform the stories you are telling yourself and get closer to the truth.

Caroline Myss, *Why People Don't Heal and How They Can* (Bantam, 1998). This book may help explain any resistance you may be having to the healing process. Lots to think about here, and her other books are also excellent.

Penny Pierce, *Frequency* (Beyond Words/Atria, Simon & Schuster, 2009). Getting bearings on your personal energy frequency and how to raise your vibration.

Lissa Rankin, *Mind over Medicine: Scientific Proof That You Can Heal Yourself* (Hay House, 2014). Written by a doctor, this book talks about how you can empower yourself as a patient and explains that there may be alternatives to traditional medicine.

Florence Scovel Shinn, *The Game of Life and How to Play It* (1925; Waiting in the Other Room Productions, 2014). The original book on manifestation and energy.

Brian Tracy, *The Psychology of Achievement* (Simon & Schuster Audio, 2002). In fact mostly anything by Brian Tracy is good for goal-setting and developing a practical positive mindset about creating a life you love.

Alberto Villoldo, *Shaman, Healer, Sage* (Bantam, 2001). Full of ways to work with energy as well as a different perspective on life.

Doreen Virtue, *The Lightworker's Way* (Hay House, 2005). A wonderful story about what it means to discover you are a healer and how it can impact on your life.

Joe Vitale, *The Awakening Course* (John Wiley & Sons, 2010), also *Zero Limits* (John Wiley & Sons, 2009). Joe looks at energy clearing and enlightenment, becoming aware and maximizing your potential to create a life you love.

Marianne Williamson, *A Return to Love* (Thorsons, 1996). The story of Marianne's journey of healing, interspersed with the philosophy of *A Course in Miracles*.

ABOUT THE AUTHOR

Abby Wynne is a Shamanic Psychotherapist and Energy Healer working in private practice in Dublin, Ireland. She teaches people how to reconnect to their heart and soul and become more available for life. Abby has published four books, recorded two CDs and offers healing meditations and sessions for download on her website. You can join Abby for online classes, such as her 21-day Raise Your Vibration Bootcamp, receive her weekly energy tips email or connect with her thriving social media community.

 AbbyEnergyHealing

 AbbyNrgHealing

 @abbynrghealing

www.abby-wynne.com

HAY HOUSE

Look within

Join the conversation about latest products, events, exclusive offers and more.

f Hay House UK

𝕏 @HayHouseUK

◉ @hayhouseuk

♥ healyourlife.com

We'd love to hear from you!